Choosing Your Lens

How White Christians
Can Become Better Allies

Tracey M. Lewis-Giggetts

Choosing Your Lens

How White Christians Can Become Better Allies

Tracey M. Lewis-Giggetts

New Season
BOOKS AND MEDIA

CHOOSING YOUR LENS
Helping White Christians Become Better Allies

NewSeason Books and Media, LLC
PO Box 1403
Havertown, PA 19083
www.nsbooksandmedia.com

Visit the author online at: www.hearttalkpodcast.com

Table of Contents

Introduction

Rules of Engagement

*"If I love you, I have to make you conscious
of the things that you do not see."*
James Baldwin

hen I started writing essays about social justice issues—particularly race, class, and gender, with an eye on how these issues intersect with faith and religion—the response was overwhelming. On one extreme were the high fives from those who had been waiting for someone to "just say it." On the other extreme was the name-calling and trolling. With the former, I'm always super careful. Like many creative people, I wrestle with the need for validation and I never want that to be a driving force in how I approach my work. And the latter? Eh. That kind of ugliness is just part of being a content creator—particularly one who writes and produces content that makes some people uncomfortable and unwilling to sit in that discomfort. There is actually nothing I can do about that. For me, what *was* interesting were those in the middle. Those who were genuinely wrestling with what I was writing. In this case, I received numerous inbox messages and FB comments from White believers asking a variation of this:

"I don't know what to do. As a white person, what do I do
about racism?"

As an act of self-care, I decided against going crazy by repeating myself to each individual's questions. Instead, I put together a list for those who were asking this question genuinely and from an authentic and sincere place. My words are a combination of things I've been saying for very long time. And as the James Baldwin quote that opens this chapter implies, it is *because* of love that I say these things.

What can White (people, Christians, churches) do about racism?

#1 – Stop asking Black people what to do about racism

Yikes.

This is probably where I should re-emphasize the fact that I'm saying this in love.

Black people have been dealing with white supremacy and racism in this land since we were brought to these shores. We have endured slavery, lynching, segregation, redlining, segregation, brutality, discrimination, and much more. To ask a group that has endured that kind of hardship, who continues to see our children shot down in the street, our churches go up in flames, and our opportunities...though vastly greater than in the past...still limited in comparison to the dominant culture, to now come up with all the solutions and directions for the very system that has caused this pain is disingenuous at best. As Toni Morrison[1] once said, *we cannot be both the doctor and the patient.* There comes a time when White people will have to reckon with and take responsibility for what has been done on their own. Yes, dialogue with Black people is important but having the hard conversations within your own communities-yes, to other White people-is becoming increasingly more important.

And I'm not clear as to why that's hard to figure out. In any other scenario, this kind of engagement is possible. In business, with other social issues, in the sciences, even in other areas of the church-caucuses are formed, dialogue is had, and solutions, good or bad, are found. In any other tragic situation, people know how to come together to serve their fellow brothers/sisters and come up with ideas and strategy (even if imperfect) on how to help; how to affect change. But for some reason, when it comes to race in America...there's this passive "we don't know what to do, you tell us what to do" perspective.

Consider this: When there's a major flood happening, a major natural disaster, no one stop and says to those who are actively dying in the disaster, "How I can help you stop a flood? Break down the ways I can help you." You simply grab some sandbags and GET TO WORK! But helping someone in a flood is risky business. And so is tackling racism. So it seems the underlying question is actually, "What can I do about racism that won't force me to risk anything in the process?" And the answer to that is...nothing. You must be willing to lay your reputation down, risk being hated, to stand up for people of color on any number of issues that can be found with a simple Google search (on top of the fact that Black folks have been screaming about them since Reconstruction.)

#2 – Try asking a better question. Here's one: how can I educate myself about the Black experience in America?

Here's the thing: now more than ever, because of the internet, White people have access to everything they need to know about Black history or the Black experience.

Enough to arm themselves when they have those conversations *with each other.*

White people also have access to ways to disseminate that information to people in their circles who might be more influential than any one individual. In your particular area and family, you might not think you "see" racism that much but as long as it exists, it's your problem too.

Sidebar: White believers, stop walking up to Black people saying, "I'm sorry that happened." Because essentially what many of us hear is, "I'm sorry that happened to YOUR people." Yet if you believe what the word of God says—"In Christ's family there can be no division into Jew and non-Jew, slave and free, male and female. Among us you are all equal..." (see Galatians 3:28)—then you understand that you don't need to apologize to me because it's happening to YOU too. The fact that you can apologize to me, as well intentioned as it might be, is further evidence of your disconnection from the problem. It's evidence of your embracing of some ideal that makes my humanity different from yours. It shows an inability to feel the deep hurt of your brother and sister–a hallmark of walking like Christ.

Okay...back to educating yourself. Once you've done some reading and gotten your questions answered about specific issues, you can now bring awareness to the issue in your own sphere of influence...especially and particularly if it's all white. As eluded to earlier, you have a social media platform, you know people, you can make calls to the media and government officials, you can set up forums at your church, you can visit a Black church or other predominately Black organizations to show solidarity, you can send money to activist organizations, you can make an effort to diversify your experiences, etc. Any white person, even someone who lives in an environment where racist activity is not seen everyday (uhhh, because it's probably all white–which is likely evidence all by itself though I digress), can be an advocate if they want to. And they can do so, without having to constantly ask Black folks, "How can I help?"

But Tracey, how do I talk to other white people about racism if I don't know your plight?

Okay, if you have educated yourself but still don't feel like you "understand" what's happening, here's our plight:

1. There are stereotypes, generalizations, and assumptions made about what it means to be a Black person that fuels the fear and hatred against us.
2. Black people are treated unfairly in our economic, education, and justice systems.
3. Too many Black people have been/are being killed or injured because they are Black.

Just start there. Own these pieces. Let the evidence of what you learn seep into you.

Don't deflect. Push down your inclination to go defensive, to trot out the exceptions, or to speak about ancillary issues ("Oh but what about Black on Black crime?") in order to make yourself feel better about what you are learning. In fact, don't center your feelings or experiences at all (No "but what about me?" responses).

You won't feel good about what you learn and you may never "understand." But there's enough pain in those two points for you to be able to go back into your community and say, "What are we going to do about this?" Brainstorming from the privileged perspective is very much needed because you may have more of the means to demand change. So a better question to ask people of color

5

than the vague "What can I do?" too often asked solely to assuage the conviction you feel, is "I want to educate myself on your history and story, could you suggest some places and resources that could help?" That shows way more intentionality than "Just tell me what to do to fix this."

A great resource is the Charleston syllabus [2]put together by a professor at Brandeis. It will seem overwhelming so I recommend you starting with the links to the Op-Eds. Anything written by Ta-nehisi Coates [3]of The Atlantic is worth digesting.

How does one demand that public school education is equal, that racist symbols and policies are not allowed to stand, that rogue police are held accountable, that there is diversity and inclusion at every level in business, that little white kids are not allowed by their parents to call my baby girl N*gger on the playground? Well, if I'm honest, I don't know if that's for Black folks to answer for you. It's time for white people to do the work and brainstorm. In the meantime, I will grieve and pray and work, work and pray and grieve.

#3 – Talk Amongst Yourselves. Then do something.

Start with your immediate circle. Start with other White people. I believe engagement looks like white people, and white believers specifically, engaging in conversations amongst themselves and strategizing on how to leverage their status to make change.

Talk to each other. YOU check your fringe elements before "Black" Twitter gets a chance to turn their words into the next meme. Leverage your privilege in order to dismantle the system. Stop asking the people who are on the receiving end of 400 years of abuse for the solution. And yes, I get that it is frustrating to hear someone say this to you when you may be sincerely wanting to help but please shift your lens a bit. This is not the time for white people to center the issue of racism on how helpless THEY feel. Imagine what it would be like to have the kind of history Black people have in this country and then be tasked with having to educate the oppressor and those who benefit from the oppression (for those of who you who say, "Well I didn't hurt anyone"). Imagine that you must bury your child who was shot and killed for walking while Black and then you are asked, "What can we do to help?"

Umm...make it stop?

Black people have fought, prayed, cried, marched, rioted, and voted to be seen as equal and valuable in the eyes of our government and its systems. If we knew how to dismantle racism, it would have been done already.

There are still way too many organizations, particularly white Christian evangelical ministries, that have quite a bit of cultural, political, and social capital who won't even DARE have the necessary conversations much less do anything about what is happening. Where are the leaders standing up demanding to know the truth about these church burnings and calling it what it is—terrorism—on Fox News no less? Who is demanding that the media and politicians talk about it seriously? If enough of those orgs as well as individuals were engaged, then the Confederate flag would be down, body cams and accountability would be a non-issue, and other issues would suddenly become much more clear. Institutional racism is not as circumstantial or unlegislated as one might think. The key is to look at circumstances and legislations through the lens of the group adversely affected.

Scary huh?! Sure it is. But be clear. Your fear doesn't exist because you don't know what to say–especially if you've educated yourself. Your fear exists because it's super risky to say anything. Courage is not something Black folks can give you. Courage is going to come from the conviction of the Holy Spirit or by God's pressing. Pray for courage.

#4 - So don't talk to Black folks at all?

Of course I'm not saying that. I think it's important to talk to people of all different backgrounds—for relational purposes. Get to know me. Black people aren't a monolith so my experience with racism will not be the same as someone else's. Same goes with the random Black person plucked from obscurity to speak on CNN or Fox News. They don't represent us all just like a Dylan Roof doesn't represent all white people. So I submit that the best route to fruitful discussions with Black people will derive from coming alongside individuals with the intention of getting to know us individually and not, necessarily, as a knee jerk reaction to current events. (Although that could be the catalyst for you to establish the relationship) And be transparent. Be authentic. Be honest about what you do and don't know. Say, "hey, this is what I think. I don't know if that's true for you. What do you think?" Engage in a dialogue—not in a one-sided "break it all down" for me conversation. Be willing to hear the hard things. Be willing to be uncomfortable with what you learn. Sit with that discomfort.

Yes, as human beings, that's hard for all of us to do. But it's still critical. In these conversations, you will likely discover, if you don't know already, that as a white person, your point of view is privileged. So what! Don't let that discovery unnerve you. Own it. Most people of color, particularly those active in this justice movement, know that already.

We get that. What we don't get is this denial or lack of acknowledging of it–especially within the Church. What we appreciate is someone who is not afraid to speak up for something that is obviously wrong...even when they may not understand all the nuances fully. We appreciate those who are willing to risk reputation and other things to stand in the gap for the disenfranchised. Whether your ancestors were slaveholders or not, you have benefited from white supremacy. And it's going to take all of us to shut it down. And its especially going to take all of us who are believers to represent Christ in the matter. So in addition to having intellectual integrity when it comes to racism by educating yourself, as a believer, ask God to illuminate areas in your life where you might be influential. Racism...and every other ism for that matter...is linked directly to the prejudiced hearts of those who have the power to oppress (and those who benefit from that power). And it's the heart that has to be healed, resurrected even, before systems can change. So I encourage you to ask God to heal your heart before embarking on the monumental task of dismantling racist systems. Otherwise, the system will simply speak to and reinforce what you already believe and you will do nothing worthwhile.

Afterward, consider where you live, how your schools are structured, the demographics of your church, how you vote. Be willing to have the hard conversations with people in your sphere of influence that may not be aware or care about justice for people of color. It will be frustrating, no doubt. Risky? Definitely. But it's so very necessary.

***

A Facebook friend shared with me that she was walking in a park right after Dylan Roof[4], a white supremacist, shot nine African American members of a church in Charleston, SC [5] in a devastating hate crime. An elderly White man

9

walked up to her and said, "On behalf of the white race, I'd like to apologize for what happened in Charleston. The white race is not like that." *There goes that apology.* My FB friend was so stunned by the man's words that she, in her nervousness most likely, chuckled. The guy left her slightly frustrated. If I had to guess, he probably said to himself, "See. I tried. I can't talk about this." Her post got me to thinking: Part of seeking justice and racial reconciliation has to also include white people being willing to acquire the language necessary to express and examine their authentic feelings about racism and racial injustice. It's not just that people don't have the I.Q. to understand what's happening. It's that people don't have the E.Q. (emotional intelligence) to process what's happening and reconcile the significant role they play in it.

My hope is that this book helps the journey toward emotional intelligence on these issues.

Are you considering not reading further? Has what I've said so far pricked you more than a little bit? That's probably a sign you should press in further. And take heart! You've made it through the toughest part.

Press past the pain and dig in. Because that's what true allies for Godly justice are called to do.

---

[1] Toni Morrison (b. 1931) is a noted American author, Nobel Laureate (Literature, 1993) and academic. Her work is revered for her ability to weave deeply complex African American characters with astute themes of race, gender, identity, politics, and American life.
http://www.biography.com/people/toni-morrison-9415590

[2] http://aaihs.org/resources/charlestonsyllabus/

3 Ta-Nehisi Coates (b. 1975) is an American writer/journalist and national correspondent for *The Atlantic*. His most recent work, *Between the World and Me* (2016) received critical acclaim for shedding light on Black male masculinity, politics, and how these areas intersect in American society. http://www.theatlantic.com/politics/archive/2016/06/black-journalist-and-the-racist-mountain/484808/

4 Dylann Roof (b. 1994) allegedly perpetrated the June 17, 2015 mass shooting at the Emanuel African Methodist Episcopal Church in Charleston, South Carolina. It is believed Roof's motivation was his disdain for African Americans, as he had been particularly outspoken about the deaths of Trayvon Martin and Freddie Gray. http://www.cnn.com/2016/11/07/us/dylann-roof-trial/

5 Charleston Massacre (June 17, 2015) was a mass shooting at Emanuel African Methodist Episcopal Church claimed the lives of: Cynthia Marie Graham Hurd, Susie Jackson, Ethel Lee Lance, Depayne Middleton-Doctor, Clementa C. Pinckney, Tywanza Sanders, Daniel Simmons, Sharonda Coleman-Singleton, and Myra Thompson. http://time.com/time-magazine-charleston-shooting-cover-story/

2

Church, your legs are burning!

"His word is in my heart like a fire, a fire shut up in my bones. I am weary of holding it in; indeed, I cannot" (Jeremiah 20:9)

The outrage bubbling just under my skin, in my heart, was near boiling. I felt just like Jeremiah. Only now, there was a literal fire.

Arson.

7 churches in the South.

7 predominantly (I'm guessing, at least, 90%) Black churches.[1]

> *In this way we are like the various parts of a human body. Each part gets its meaning from the body as a whole, not the other way around. The body we're talking about is Christ's body of chosen people. Each of us finds our meaning and function as a part of his body. But as a chopped-off finger or cut-off toe we wouldn't amount to much, would we? So since we find ourselves fashioned into all these excellently formed and marvelously functioning parts in Christ's body, let's just go ahead and be what we were made to be... – Romans 12:4-6a (MSG)*

Insanity. The Body was burning and the Church seemed to collectively refuse to stop, drop and roll.

It was like having arthritis in my left arm, someone coming along and setting my sleeve on fire, and me refusing to put the fire out because *"Oh that arm is such a pain anyway. Always hurting!"* Fool, don't you know that the fire will consume you too!
(Although I must say that my analogy doesn't work entirely. Arthritis isn't an inflicted pain like racism, so there's that.)

Church, a portion of our Body is on fire? Will we let it burn?

"Oh the church is the people; these are just buildings. We can rebuild."

Yes, we can rebuild church buildings. But when I say "your legs are on fire" it's not just the church buildings I'm talking about—it's the PEOPLE. Fearfully and wonderfully, made in the image of God, PEOPLE.

> *But if anyone has the world's goods and sees his brother in need, yet closes his heart against him, how does God's love abide in him? Little children, let us not love in word or talk but in deed and in truth. – 1 John 3:17-18 ESV*

Black and Brown folks are burning. Seems like every day, we are dying, ultimately, from a white supremacist system that gives birth to a Dylan Roof, the KKK and numerous rogue cops. A system that too many of our alleged white brothers and sisters in Christ are complicit in.

Yes, complicit.

Consciously or unconsciously, you enable racist acts daily when you choose to do nothing in the face of them. When you refuse to acknowledge, let alone leverage your privilege to dismantle the system. When, instead of caucusing and coming up with your own solutions, you passive aggressively ask Black folks *"What can I do about racism?"* as if we are the ones who created it. When you can compartmentalize Charleston and these burnings as something that's happening "down there" to "those people."

I'm curious. What would happen if white, conservative, evangelical churches in the north started burning?

> *This just in from our news desk: 7 predominately white churches have been set on fire. But it may not be hate crime. Investigators must rule out faulty wiring because the likelihood of 7 churches with the same demographics across multiple states burning down because of electrical issues within two weeks of a mass murder of 9 white folks in a church is...oh wait, in other news...gay marriage has passed.*

Yeah. Exactly. Sit with that for a minute.

Sit with it and realize that if you and your local church would respond differently in my fictional scenario than what's REALLY happening with your black and brown brothers and sisters in the faith, then you, Sir or Ma'am, have some serious reckoning to do.

The trick of the enemy from the dawn of this country is to position white people to believe that they can facilitate (actively or passively) the social, economic, and yes, physical burning of Black bodies and communities and think they won't be burnt in the process.

> *Because the king was in such a hurry and the furnace was so hot, flames from the furnace killed the men who carried Shadrach, Meshach, and Abednego to it, while the fire raged around Shadrach, Meshach, and Abednego. – Daniel 3:23, MSG*

As followers of Jesus, we are called to function as one Body. Period. So to white believers who refuse to engage, whose eyes remained veiled, I hate to break it to you: the racist "fire" embedded in our systems and culture (King), that tries to consume your Black and Brown brothers and sisters, will be the fire that consumes YOU too!

Oh grace us like your servants, Lord!

So keep being silent if you want to, Church!

Keep letting the media INSTEAD of the Holy Spirit define for you what's happening and guide your response. The American church's silence/neutrality on, and in some cases, denial of, the powder keg called race in America— this "let's pray, forgive, and that's it" approach with no push for accountability, no significant response outside of the alleged safety of the pulpit—absolutely lights the match on the next church.

And the next one could be yours.

---

[1] In the aftermath of the Charleston Massacre, several predominately Black churches across the American southeast and Midwest became targets of white supremacists groups. These church burnings inspired the hash tag

#whoisburningblackchurches. There were no reported fatalities during these incidents.

http://www.pri.org/stories/2015-07-02/fire-last-time-1990s-wave-145-church-burnings-map

3

Of Flagpoles and Fearlessness

"I tell you the truth, if you had faith even as small as a mustard seed, you could say to this mountain, 'Move from here to there,' and it would move. Nothing would be impossible." -Matthew 17:20b, NLT

All paths come with obstacles. All roads will eventually lead through roadblocks and tollbooths, construction and detours. In my part of the country, those "blocks" might include a mountain or five. But no one driving west from Philly says, "Welp, can't go to Chicago because of all those mountains in the way." Nope, we keep driving. When our intricate network of interstates were built, the mountains were carefully considered and evaluated, but not a one stopped the work.

And so it goes with our lives. There will certainly be mountains. Monstrous obstacles that seem to impede our progress. And we will certainly be called to evaluate the role these mountains play in our journey; we must consider the risks and costs. Particularly, white allies for racial justice, supporting thousands of black and brown activists, must not allow the mountain of white supremacy (we'll talk more about that in the next chapter) to prevent you from pressing forward.

What does "pressing forward" look like?

There will be times when we'll have to climb over a mountain. Other times, we'll have to take some extra time and go around it. But I believe that God calls some us to a radical, fearless approach. Some of us will have to, like those who constructed the Pennsylvania Turnpike, BLAST right through the middle of that thing in our way.

Ask Bree Newsome.[1]

Bree is the woman who, in a fearless act of civil disobedience, scaled a flagpole in South Carolina to remove the Confederate flag[2] —a symbol of a lost war and the dehumanization of black people through enslavement.

Sure, she could have gone around that mountain. Although this is the long way to change, she could have avoided places where such racist symbols and icons exist. Not spend her money in places that support injustice. She could have turned the channel when some random pseudo-pundit is spewing hatred or ignorance. Those are important measures that many will take in order to protect their sanity and mental health.

These are all valid ways to press forward.

She also could have taken the tedious route of going over the mountain. She could have signed petitions, marched on Washington, and done any number of things to express the outrage that so many of us have over what that flag represents–in a way that is societally appropriate and legal. This is also an effective move. We need people who are going to call out the system, infiltrate it even; those who will work as lawyers and activists to bring about change.

These are also valid ways to press forward.

But Bree's task was different. Still very strategic, but much more direct.

Climb the pole. Remove the offense.

I know, I know. You're thinking, *well, what good did that do? They just put right back up.*

Of course they did. That wasn't the point. The point was to make a statement that would reverberate and resonate throughout this country. To maximize the viral nature of social media and have her act playing over and over again on the screens and in the minds of people. You see, how many people who experience racism and injustice on a daily basis, who watched this Black woman calmly climb that flagpole, recite scripture, and remove that flag, will now feel emboldened and empowered to stand up for RIGHT and JUSTICE in their own neighborhoods and communities?

How many writers like myself, who can sometimes feel the weight of our particular callings, will press on another day to use our pens to shed light on issues that matter?

How many of you will begin to look for opportunities to tear down racism in your own circles as a result of watching this one woman's courage?

So in that way, I suppose, Bree not only blasted through her own proverbial mountain but the obstacles of complacency and fear that stand in the way of many of us who are exhausted, grieved, or clueless.

See, many of us are called to blow up mountains of injustice...not with sticks of dynamite...but with powerful acts of righteous defiance. Like Jesus did the moneychangers in the Temple (see John 2:15), we are called to drive out those who dare to defile and cheat and disparage others who are made in the image of God. It's not an easy calling, for sure. And some of that "blowing up" may not make it to Facebook and television. Maybe your act of righteous defiance is demanding that your local public school system be a suitable place for children to learn (instead of snatching your kids out and doing nothing). Or maybe you are called to stand armed on the street corners ensuring that drug dealers don't set up shop (instead of moving away because YOU can). Maybe you must demand accountability from the police officers in your neighborhood; filming their behavior every chance you get until they change.

To a certain extent, I wonder if we all, at some point, must be willing to risk our reputations and livelihoods for the greater good. As Mark 8:36 says: *For what does it profit a man to gain the whole world and forfeit his soul?*

Do we lose our souls if all we do is, while watching the magnified intensity of hatred against Black and Brown bodies nowadays, pay lip service to the 'tragedy' within the comfort and privacy of our homes and churches?

I ask myself this: what mountain will I go over, around, or through today? What flagpole will I climb?

I ask you the same.

---

[1] Bree (ne. Brittany Ann) Newsome (b. mid-1980's) is a musician, documentarian, and activist most noted for scaling the flagpole in front of the South Carolina statehouse to remove the Confederate flag. https://www.washingtonpost.com/news/arts-and-entertainment/wp/2015/06/28/who-is-bree-newsome-why-the-woman-who-took-down-the-confederate-flag-became-an-activist/

[2] Confederate Flag Controversy (2015) shed light on/re-ignited the debate surrounding the historic significance and meaning of the Confederate flag in America. Proponents suggest the flag is part of American tradition and southern identity, while others stress its racist iconography. http://www.cbsnews.com/videos/s-c-statehouse-fights-over-confederate-flag-controversy/

4

Where in the HELL are you, Church?

Yes, I meant that.

No, the title of this chapter is not a mistake.

I'm really asking.

Church, where in *all this hell* are you?

Because when Black bodies that look scarily similar to my child's, my husband's, and mine are regularly burned and broken, it feels like a raging, unholy hell to me. So let's not mince words. Let's call it exactly what it is.

And just so I don't die a slow psychological and spiritual death as a result of what seems like the complete and utter impotence of the church, I must lay my burdens on this altar of words and openly discuss the struggles I'm having with many in the Faith—Black and White—who seem unaffected or downright antagonistic when it comes to issues of race.

Here's a truth that might be hard for some to swallow: There's a link between Minnesota, Charleston and McKinney[1] and Baltimore[2] and Ferguson[3] and Tamir Rice [4] and Eric Garner [5] and Trayvon Martin [6] and Breonna Taylor and George Floyd. This link is a kind of thread that is both old and strong. It's the same thread that linked Amadou Diallo[7] and James Byrd [8]and Emmett Till[9] and the burning of Black Wall Street[10] and the lynchings of Black people[11] in the South. And the first knot in the thread, the threading of the needle if you will, happened along the middle passage during the transatlantic slave trade [12]. Because this thread has proven itself lucrative over the last 400 years, it has never been cut off.

Some folks think my "thread" metaphor is too generous. When I discussed this essay with Writer, Minister, Filmmaker, and dear friend of mine, Alexus Rhone, she pulled no punches in her assessment:

You call it a "thread" Tracey, but I call it a demonic spirit imbued within the fabric of a nation too proud to bend in humility and mourn the sins of their fathers that have literally been passed down to their children. Instead of exorcising the demons, they've signed peace treaties with them.

To be clear: the thread I'm talking about, the demonic spirit Alexus is talking about, is *White supremacy*. And the manifestation of its presence is exactly what we are seeing today; the evidence that Black lives really don't matter. And before you begin to compartmentalize it, let me go ahead and say this: This thread of White supremacy runs through the fabric of EVERY American institution that exists, including—dare I say it—the American church.

The deafening silence of the Body of Christ *as a collective* on the recent injustices against people color here in the U.S. and around the world (see Dominican Republic[13]), to me, is evidence of the insidious, cancerous infiltration of racism and white supremacy in our Body.

That he might present it to himself a glorious church, not having spot, or wrinkle, or any such thing; but that it should be holy and without blemish. – Ephesians 5:27 KJV

Jesus isn't coming for perfect individuals but He is coming for a Church that is unified in its awareness of its Blood washed sins and has accomplished His mission with all the grace He did on earth. He's coming for a Church that, at a very basic level, has maintained the two greatest commandments: To love God and to love our neighbors as ourselves. Unfortunately, because the institution of the Church is just as divided as this country, we remain as spotted, wrinkled and blemished as anything else.

And it is deeply affecting our witness to the world.

Let's think about this from even an evangelistic perspective: there are thousands, if not millions, of unbelievers who are directly and indirectly affected by systemic racism. If the Body of Christ stood unified and willing to fight this evil, not on the basis that we agree on every political or social issue, but on the basis that we follow the same Jesus who died on the cross for every single one of us and commanded that we stand up for those who are considered the "least," what message would that send to a dying, sin-sick world?

What an amazing act of love that would be. (The South African Truth and Reconciliation Commission[14] is one of a few godly models of what this looks like).

But...for some—most likely White Christians—even my using the phrase "white supremacy" probably has your chest heaving. You're anxious. You are ready to scroll down right now and let loose on the comments section with all the reasons why I've conjured up the concept or why you're tired of "people like me" playing the race card because everything isn't about "race" and good Christians know this.

Some of you might even have turned up your favorite cable news channel in order to allow all the ridiculous side-stepping and out and out lies about the racist disposition of #McKinney or #Charleston or any of the other tragic events of the last couple of years to somehow drown out my words and the accountability and conviction they raise in you. You've created templates of justification that you copy and paste all over social media in order to reconcile your hatred, your denial or your complacency.

On one point, you're right though. Everything isn't about race. Some things are. Given the history of our country, many things are. And on those many things, I tend to play the cards how they're dealt.

Consider this: if you find yourself sitting in your home and hearing about nine Black people in a church Bible Study being killed because of a murderous terrorist's false belief that Black people are somehow "taking over the country," and your only response is to find a justification OTHER than racism—you don't shed one tear, your spirit doesn't rage with a desire for justice, you don't see the blatant disparities in how this suspect was treated as opposed to any of the Black men and women who encounter police, you don't even bow your head in prayer to ask God to send his Holy Spirit to comfort those who have lost their loved ones—yeah, you might want to check your heart real quick and see if Jesus really lives there. Because this:

> *Be happy with those who are happy, and weep with those who weep.* – Romans 12:15

And this:

> *Blessed be the God and Father of our Lord Jesus Christ, the Father of mercies and God of all comfort, who comforts us in all our affliction, so that we may be able to comfort those who are in any affliction, with the comfort with which we ourselves are comforted by God.* – 2 Corinthians 1:3-4

And this:

> *Bear one another's burdens, and so fulfill the law of Christ.* – Galatians 6:2

And worse, if you are a church leader, and your first impulse wasn't to contact or connect with other churches down in Charleston, to find out what was needed and how you and your congregation can stand in solidarity with the Black community against the kind of individual and systemic racism that gives birth to a Dylan Roof, then, to you, I would also suggest thinking long and hard about how you are walking out your call.

Because this:

> *My brethren, let not many of you become teachers, knowing that we shall receive a stricter judgment.* – James 3:1

But for my white brothers and sisters in the Faith who have made it this far in this chapter—in this book—and still genuinely want to know how to be a part of a united and collective reconciliation effort, allow me to help you to dig a little deeper for the sake of understanding. RobtheIdealist of Orchestrated Pulse does a great job of defining white supremacy for any white person who may not "get it."

In order to have a productive conversation on oppression, it is important to recognize that the key factor is superiority. In any caste system there is a group that believes itself superior (which by default assumes the inferiority of any "Other"), creates systemic advantages for itself, and then uses violence to ensure its dominance.

So, in the case of racism, the supremacist ideology that anchors the system is called "white supremacy". Racism is a white supremacist ideology backed by systemic power, and reinforced through violence.

We so often want to speak in terms of who *is*and isn't racist, thus treating racism as an individual state of being, rather than a system of power. Racism is not merely a personal attitude or an insult; instead, it's a racial system of power maintained by violence (with the violence often going unpunished because it is protected by the dominant system of power). Therefore, an individual can be perpetuating this system without even being conscious of their actions.

Ultimately, we are all complicit in the perpetuation of systemic white supremacy, but we are not all equally culpable, nor do we all benefit equally. When we talk about white supremacy, we must make sure that the discussion is multidimensional.

That's a lot to process for some. Particularly believers who, on the one hand, prefer to think that with salvation came some kind of transcendence over these racist systems, yet on the other hand, benefit from those systems daily.

***

I'm comfortable acknowledging that what's happened over the last few years has been heavy. It has been. But none of what you're seeing is new. African Americans and other peoples of color have been experiencing this kind of brutality at the hands of whites since Columbus figured out he actually wasn't in India and those thousands of people already living here weren't Indians. Fortunately, social media has been able to shine a big bright ugly light on what has been a common experience for those in Black communities.

Yes, social media, with all its ills, has served as technological mirror for our society. A mirror that reflects a truth so ugly that so many of my white brothers and sisters in the Faith have chosen to sweep it under the proverbial rug. This truth reveals to some that they worship and serve in cities that might be highly diverse and yet their immediate worlds are not. This truth reveals that most believe that it is the "Black church" and a few select white activists' responsibility to deal with all that *civil rights stuff.* This truth reveals that some still have antiquated notions of how to engage those who different (Bringing LeCrae [15]to a once a year youth conference but never truly connecting with the demographic he represents, DOES NOT COUNT).
This truth also exposes the inner workings of individual hearts. Hearts that don't have a problem serving rice to the inner city poor at a soup kitchen but who wouldn't dream of inviting those same people into their homes. Hearts that

don't have a problem with integrated schools or pools as long as they are never outnumbered and their daughters and sons don't bring "one" home.

If you have children, look at them right now, and sit with that.

See, this thing is sooo beyond just "those people" wanting social justice. *Those people* are your brothers and sisters in humanity. When people who call themselves Christ-followers stop really *seeing* people and decide to replace human beings with stereotypes and caricatures gathered from a biased and agenda-driven media, it makes the decision to not stand for right seem, well, right. When Eric Garner becomes just another lazy, fat, Black guy standing on the corner selling cigarettes instead of maybe a hard-working father talking to friends in his community and making a couple of extra dollars for his family...and that image is used to justify his death... there is, without a doubt, a deep heart problem.

> *For the word of God is living and powerful, and sharper than any two-edged sword, piercing even to the division of soul and spirit, and of joints and marrow, and is a discerner of the thoughts and intents of the heart. And there is no creature hidden from His sight, but all things are naked and open to the eyes of Him to whom we must give account. – Hebrews 4:12-13 NKJV*

Oh and Black folks in the Faith, we aren't off the hook here. That same mirror has reflected some pretty awful truths in us. Mostly that some of us have internalized the lies handed down in slavery that we are inferior and many of us, mostly our men, are inherently criminal.

I do think though that some of that internalized enablement of white supremacy is a kind of defense mechanism. See most Black folks I know firmly believed that the rights fought for by our mothers and fathers during the civil rights movement meant something. We had hope that, in time, we would one day be seen as equal and valuable.

But it's been more than 50 years and we are finding with every new video and case, that maybe, just maybe that might not be true. Some of us are surprised. Some of us aren't. But one too many of us have chosen oblivion because it's easier to keep the pain at bay. To not lose our minds. We think that as long as we stay blind and talk about Black-on-Black crime, we can somehow remain respectable and on the good sides of our white friends and fellow believers. We, as Walter Brueggemann says, fall into one two groups: "those who are numb" and "those who despair." The "numb" group insulates themselves so that they don't feel anything. But in order for them to act, they will need to be pierced by grief. The "despairing" group feels all the heaviness AND the powerlessness and just wallow in despair. What they need is a language that communicates hope for the future.

It's a lot, I know. Exposure, whether it's of the state of our own hearts or the larger systems pulling us down, is heavy. The country feels like it is on the brink of civil war. And yet, the one group that can handle what's happening, that should be spiritually armed with both the power and grace from a Sovereign AND Warrior God (see Exodus 15), has decided to lay back and be seized by the enemy. Who in the Faith are truly caucusing on these issues? No one seems to be willing to make the sacrifices of the Acts church. How many of us are willing to be true Apostles and have our material and yes even physical lives martyred for standing on the side of right?

I'm struggling with that too.

And yes, I understand that, as believers, our first instinct is to pray. It should be. That's a good start. But uh oh, what happens after we pray? In fact, what exactly are we asking God for? *Thy will be done* is a given. But isn't prayer also about receiving our marching orders? Guidance and direction from the One who sees the end from the beginning? White brothers and sisters, are you really ready to ask God to deliver true equality into the hands of people of color in this country, knowing full well what that might require you to do AND what that might mean for your own status? Black brothers and sisters, are you ready for the accountability and responsibility that comes with justice and equality? If your answers to these questions are yes, then great! However, I suspect that the answers to the next question might be infinitely harder to grasp.

What does His will regarding this gaping wound of White supremacy in America look like?

Well...what if His will is for the Church to take a stand? To shout from the rooftops, my white brothers and sisters, that systemic racism and all its offspring (police brutality, discrimination) is wrong and won't be tolerated whether it shows up on a flag pole on a state capital building (!) or in our very own pulpits. What if His will, Black brothers and sisters, is for you to put down your self-hating "I made it, why can't you?" pseudo-righteousness and your "It will get better bye and bye" complacency and stand alongside those—yes, even unbelievers—who are marching the streets on behalf of all our futures?

As the disciples used to say to our Lord, "this is a hard saying, who can hear it?" (see John 6:60)

And yeah, I get it. There's this natural, human tendency to run away from the hard stuff. The stuff that makes us uncomfortable. The stuff that challenges our notions of who we are, who others are, the systems we work and live in, and what God is calling us to do. But how is it that, in times past (see Slavery, Reconstruction, Civil Rights era), our same deep need for justice to prevail and for compassion to rule, was able to live alongside our need for self-preservation and yet, the former still won out? What has changed, People of God? It was a battle then and it's a battle now, for sure. All wranglings with the flesh are. But the one thing that usually gave "right" and "love" the edge in our internal wars was this sense that we belonged to each other. That we lived in this outpost of Eden together and that even the worst of us was connected to us somehow.

This, I believe, is where true Faith lives.

And yet here we are. Men, women and children are being murdered and, for the most part, the Church is absent.

Well we aren't totally absent. Many of us will show up when those who are dealing with this pain, this generations-long disenfranchisement decide to turn to rioting. When we feel threatened, when there's a possibility that the rage will hit too close to our safe havens and disrupt our status quos, then we have a whole lot to say.
Writer, scholar, and white, social justice activist, Tim Wise, had a response to such "sudden concern" that was more powerful than anything I could write.

If your concerns about violence are limited to property damage and looting, and you have never shed two tears for the history of institutional violence, murder, colonialism, segregation, lynching, genocide and police brutality against peoples of color, your words mean nothing; they mean less than nothing. Your outrage, in such a case is grotesque, an inversion of morality so putrescent as to call into question your capacity for real feeling at all. So long as violence from below is condemned while violence from above is ignored, you can bet that the former will continue–and however unfortunate that may be, it is surely predictable. If you'd like the former to cease, put an end to the latter, and then I promise you, it will.

I know, I know, YOUR church had a march just last week, right? I'm not talking to you, right?

I would certainly be remiss to suggest that there are no churches out on the forefront of these issues. Of course there are. But sadly, there are still waaaay too many who will conduct an entire worship service this Sunday and not mention ONE WORD about what they plan to DO to help Emanuel AME or about what's happening in our country at all. In fact, there's even a segment of so-called Christians who will castigate pastors and ministry leaders who do engage by saying they shouldn't get involved in such activities because… I don't know…demanding justice is not biblical? Anger should be channeled SOLELY through prayer? I suppose they forgot about the righteous anger our Savior displayed:

"Jesus entered the temple courts and drove out all who were buying and selling there. He overturned the tables of the money changers and the benches of those selling doves." – Matthew 21:12

Yes, there is such a thing as righteous anger.
This is also not to say that there haven't been white Christians speaking out. Many white allies have been involved in the fight for justice. There are always abolitionists among us and I'm grateful for that. But today, so many of the White allies I know of, are not believers. Where are you who share my faith? And when does just speaking out even become rote? See...when simply having a cop car pull up behind my husband, daughter and I at a stop light has me in near tears—not because we're doing anything wrong but because whether we are doing anything wrong might not matter—well, I wonder if we are long past white folks posting their outrage on FaceBook and going about their lives as usual. The next step is probably for every white person, and especially every white believer, to risk leveraging their privilege to dismantle the systems. Starting on your jobs, in your schools, and yes, in your churches.

As I said, there *are* some Black churches that are on the frontlines of this thing. But I wonder if the reason why there aren't more as we've seen in previous movements is also telling. Please understand that our churches are made up of men and women who are grieving and exhausted; a people who are filled with all the sorrow and frustration that comes from having America jab it's middle finger of injustice into our never healed wounds. While I don't know how effective it is, I'm not inclined to knock pastors who preach peace and prayer as the only response or teach Piein-the-Sky-Bye-and-Bye, because I understand that they too are trying to keep the pain at bay.

So, in truth, we need everybody on deck. We need white, brown, yellow and anything in-between to link arms with us and help us stand. To support us. To use whatever influence you have to effect change and *lean in* on the powers that be.
Otherwise, I'm afraid our only alternative will be to *lean* on insurrection.

> *Blessed be the Lord, my rock, who trains my hands for war, and my fingers for battle –*
> *Psalm 144:1*

Tough to read, I know.

Bottom line, the Church as a unified collective needs to sacrifice whatever narrative we are holding on to that's preventing us from standing up for people of color. Would you put it all on the line for me, Brother? Would you stand with me, Sister, if it means that you will be heckled by those white-washed tombs you call your own? Like Jesus was heckled by His own? Will you mourn when I mourn and cry when I cry? Brothers and Sisters, though you might not understand why I'm crying fully, though you may never completely know my pain, though you might not even be sure if you think I should be crying...the fact that I am crying, the fact that my heart aches, the fact that my babies are dying in the streets...is that enough for you to walk alongside me?

The biggest challenge with all this is actually an issue of spiritual proportions. All that's happening in America right now is truly an object lesson in the perils of idolatry. The rape and sexual assaults of women and children, the deaths of multiple young unarmed Black men going unaccounted for, the compassionless ranting of alleged conservatives with hiding-in-plain-site political agendas...all of this exists because we have chosen to make idols of men. Too many people, including those who profess Christ, have raised police officers and celebrities and government officials and political affiliations (on both sides of the aisle) above the knowledge of God, above the love and grace of Christ Jesus that's available, and above what the Holy Spirit is showing and prompting us to do and be in this earth. And as long as we continue to do this, we are bound to never be able to rightly discern the truth and stand for what Christ stands for. We will remain impotent.

---

1 McKinney Pool Party Incident (2015) captured, on video, a police officer's aggressive physical interactions with several African American teens attending a graduation pool party at the Craig Ranch Community North Pool in McKinney, Texas.
http://www.nbcnews.com/news/us-news/mckinney-frets-about-image-cop-video-ignites-charges-racism-n371836

2 Baltimore Uprising (2015) occurred following the death of Freddie Gray in Baltimore, Maryland. Community members, activists, and allies from across the nation gathered to peaceably protest police brutality and injustice.
http://baltimoreuprising2015.org/

3 Ferguson Protests (2014) occurred following the police shooting death of Michael Brown. These protests became the catalyst for the Black Lives Matter movement.
http://www.huffingtonpost.com/pastor-mike-mcbride/ferguson-uprising-from-a- b 8189742.html

4 Tamir Rice (2002-2014) was a 12 year-old, African American fatally shot by White police officer, Timothy Loehmann, in Cleveland, Ohio on November 22, 2014. He was carrying an airsoft replica of a handgun.
http://www.gq.com/story/tamir-rice-story

5 Eric Garner (1970-2014) was a New York City resident who died after police officers, Daniel Pantaleo and Justin Damico, used a compression chokehold to subdue him. Viral video of Garner's police interaction and subsequent death inspired the hash tag #icantbreathe.
http://www.nbcnewyork.com/news/local/Eric-Garner-Death-Chokehold-Investigation-272043511.html

[6] Trayvon Martin (1995-2012) was a 17 year-old, African American fatally shot by George Zimmerman, a volunteer for his neighborhood watch organization in Sanford, Florida on February 26, 2012. Martin was unarmed. http://www.nytimes.com/interactive/2012/04/02/us/the-events-leading-to-the-shooting-of-trayvon-martin.html?_r=0

[7] Amadou Diallo (1975-1999) was a 23 year-old Guinean immigrant who was fatally shot 19 times by plain-clothes police officers outside of his home in the Bronx, New York on the morning of February 9, 1999. Officers claimed, Diallo matched the description of a suspected rapist and had reached for a gun upon questioning. Diallo was unarmed. http://www.nytimes.com/1999/02/05/nyregion/officers-in-bronx-fire-41-shots-and-an-unarmed-man-is-killed.html

[8] James Byrd (1949-1998) was a 49 year-old African-American who was murdered by three White men on June 7, 1998 in Jasper, Texas. Byrd had accepted a ride from the men, who subsequently chained him to the back of their truck and dragged him until his head was severed. https://www.texasobserver.org/long-road-out-of-jasper/

[9] Emmitt Till (1941-1955) was a 14 year-old African-American boy visiting his family in Money, Mississippi. He was lynched on August 28, 1955 for allegedly flirting with a White woman. http://www.history.com/this-day-in-history/the-death-of-emmett-till

[10] Black Wall Street (Greenwood; Tulsa, Oklahoma) was one of the most successful and wealthiest communities in America during the 1900's. It was the locale of several prominent African-American businesses. During the 1921 Tulsa Race Riot, the community was burned to the ground by a group of Whites. http://www.ebony.com/black-history/the-destruction-of-black-wall-street-405

[11] Lynching (v. /n.): was a popular form of killing (usually by hanging) perpetuated throughout American society and often targeted African-Americans for a wide variety of perceived and actual offenses without a trial. http://www.pbs.org/wgbh/amex/till/peopleevents/e_lynch.html

[12] Transatlantic Slave Trade (1400s-1800s) was the process by which millions of captive Africans were forcibly transported into enslavement for work on American plantations, in homes, and/or sold. http://witf.pbslearningmedia.org/resource/18042ab6-0245-438a-90b0-ad12286dc308/slavery-crash-course-us-history-13/ http://www.whitneyplantation.com/the-atlantic-slave-trade.html

[13] Ethnic Cleansing in the Dominican Republic (2015-2016) has roots in 1937 Parsley Massacre conducted by then dictator Rafael Trujillo, which separated the citizens of Hispaniola, based on skin color and sowed seeds of anti-Haitian sentiment. In recent years, this sentiment has resulted in citizenship denial, mass deportation, and other forms of disenfranchisement. https://www.washingtonpost.com/news/worldviews/wp/2015/06/16/the-bloody-origins-of-the-dominican-republics-ethnic-cleansing-of-haitians/

[14] South African Truth and Reconciliation Commission (TRC) was established in 1995 following the official end of apartheid in the country. The commission sought to mediate the effects of apartheid by voicing perspectives on both sides and shedding light on potential human rights violations. https://www.britannica.com/topic/Truth-and-Reconciliation-Commission-South-Africa

[15] LaCrae (ne. Lecrae Moore; b. 1979) is an African American, Christian lyricist, musician, and author. He first garnered national recognition when is album, *Rebel* (2008) reached number one on the Billboard Gospel charts. In 2015, Lecrae released his memoir, *Unashamed.* http://www.theatlantic.com/entertainment/archive/2014/10/lecrae-christians-have-prostituted-art-to-give-answers/381103/

5

The Language of the Unheard

Author and scholar, Malcolm Gladwell, defines a "tipping point" as the moment when an idea, trend, or social behavior crosses a threshold, tips, and spreads like wildfire. Collective Rage has a tipping point. Collective Frustration has a tipping point. Social media and technology is—thankfully—shining a glaring light on a problem that has existed for generations in this country: the systemic devaluing of Black lives. And yes (because I know some are quick to point it out) that same light also reveals internal challenges within communities of color but these issues–things like Black on Black crime, education disparities, poverty– are 9 times out of 10 the residue of longstanding white supremacy. Pick one or name another and I can trace it directly to 250 years of slavery, 100 years of Jim Crow[1], and 50 years of minute progress that sure, changed behaviors, but never altered hearts and minds. This same glaring light will continue to burn bright and bold whether in Ferguson, NYC, Baltimore, or–gasp!–your neighborhood next. To what end? I honestly don't know. But pretending like you don't see what is illuminated by the light will soon no longer be an option. God help us all.

There have been several of what I call frequently asked questions and comments posted on social media attempting to make sense of what's happening. Here are my responses:

"I'm seeing too much violence coming from these so-called protestors. There are nothing but thugs and troublemakers out there."

Remember...images played over and over again on corporate owned TV networks are RARELY indicative of what's happening on the ground. The violence that you are seeing is not as large of an occurrence as the media makes it out to be with it's continuous looping of the same four or five scenes. Trust. The police (many of whom have been shown provoking violence) know this. WE are the ones who don't know that. WE are the ones why buy the repeated images on TV as the whole truth. WE are the ones who are way too concerned about respectability and "looking a certain way" to "them." So much so that we somehow cannot fathom why the Freddie Gray[2] incident would set folks who already have nothing to lose off.

But Freddie Gray was a criminal. I wouldn't want him in my neighborhood.

Not the point. IF Freddie Gray was involved in criminal activity, then he should be tried according to his crime. Unfortunately, he will not get a chance to do that. So the point of him being a criminal is moot. Does being a criminal automatically sentence you to death? If so, there are some politicians and corporate owners who should be six feet under. Here's the point: A white man with the same or worse criminal history would be alive today. Period. And THAT'S the problem. If you are someone who cannot, for whatever reason that blinds you, see that...well than sadly, you are a conspirator in the perpetuation of the brutality. And I know..."just get a job," "don't commit crimes and the police won't arrest you," "get an education." First, as many of the cases show, you don't have to have committed a crime to be a victim of police brutality or racist violence (see Zekia Boyd [3] , etc.). Second, while personal accountability is important, systemic racism, white supremacy, and even this kind of "well, I never hurt anybody" privilege makes all these "solutions" (education, etc) challenging to many populations of Black and Brown people.

Well, rioting isn't the answer. Violence is never the answer.

In a general sense, this is true. However, those who are uncomfortable or outraged with random rioting in Baltimore are often the same people who don't see any problem with strategic war–particularly when there is a dictatorship or lives at stake. (see Iraq, Afghanistan, and any other major war of the 20th/21st centuries). So is that what you'd prefer? A strategic, calculated, organized WAR against the systemic racism that has, for too long, allowed for police brutality and the devaluing of Black lives? I'm sure there are those who'd be willing to accommodate your preference since you plug your ears, hide your eyes, or use images to shift the narrative when peaceful protest and civil disobedience is the tactic of choice.

Scholar, writer, and filmmaker, Yaba Blay once said, "when it was Egypt, you called it revolution. When it is Baltimore, you call it a riot. If you had no questions about why Egyptians were burning [stuff] down in their own communities, ask no questions about Baltimore. Chew your words well before you swallow them."

Doesn't rioting and violence overshadow what those who are peacefully protesting are trying to do?

It only overshadows because WE allow it to. Because we don't hold the media accountable for the images. Because we allow the narrative to shift. Because people are quick to post their outrage at riots but are hesitant to post outrage about police brutality, etc. WE can influence the winners of *The Voice* and *American Idol* but we can't influence this particular narrative? Nah. Not buying it.

So what's the bottom line?

A drowning man will never relax. Especially when he is being held under water. It is much easier to just let go of his head than to force him into the most unnatural of actions. The human reaction to drowning is to fight until you can't breathe anymore.

So here's a thought: let go of our heads. Allies, use your privilege to pry the hands of the system off of our heads!

Riots and other violent actions are weeds that have very clear roots. Systemic racism, White Supremacy and privilege. Stop picking the weed! DIG UP THE ROOT!
White allies and the Body of Christ–yes, the Church–get off your hands; stop hiding behind your Twitter handles and political affiliations and get some courage! You need to have as much of a righteous anger about this as people of color in these communities. Force accountability. Put your words out there. Put your support out there.

Then pray.

---

[1] Jim Crow Laws (1890s-1960s) were state and local laws enacted throughout America (especially in the South) after the abolishment of slavery to further disenfranchise and disinherit Blacks. These laws were used to limit African American agency in transportation, voting, home/business ownership, land purchase, and education, among other areas.
http://www.ferris.edu/jimcrow/what.htm

[2] Freddie Gray (1989-2015) was a 25 year-old African American man who was arrested by Baltimore City police officers for carrying a switchblade on

April 12, 2015. While in police custody, Gray suffered numerous injuries and fell into a coma. His death was ruled a homicide.
http://www.bbc.com/news/world-us-canada-32400497

[3] Rekia Boyd (1990-2012) was a 22 year-old African American woman who was fatally shot by an off-duty police officer in Chicago, Illinois on March 21, 2012. The police officer, Dante Servin, shot into a group of partygoers and a bullet to Boyd's head killed her.
http://bigstory.ap.org/article/840e7c16e92b47a488dfec2adcb7c316/chicago-officer-who-killed-unarmed-woman-resigns-force

INTERMISSION

Meeting Mae Green
(a short story)

Insecurity leaps from the woman's eyes when I nod my request to sit in her row. Just jumps right out at me, landing square between mine. In one quick move, she unbuckles her seatbelt and hurls herself from the window seat to the cramped middle one saying—as if it hurt to even fix her mouth to acknowledge me—"I'm with him."

I mean seriously, what does she really think will happen if I sit next to her husband on the plane? Will all my fabulousness become so overwhelming to him that a torrid love affair will ensue right before her eyes? All within the span of a two and a half hour flight, no less?

Hmph!

Honey, I *wish* I had that kind of persuasion. I can think of a whole bunch of stuff I'd have in my life if I did, none of which would be some dried up white man that looks like he is only two days from being in the grave.

Lord ha' mercy! I know I'm wrong for saying something like that. Shoot, that man has at least a couple of years.

Anyway, her fear, the candy-coated kind, where smiles never quite reach the eyes, is actually pretty entertaining. It's most certainly helping me keep my mind off of this terrible turbulence rocking and rolling my stomach something awful. Maybe this is the rollercoaster route to the East Coast or something, I don't know. They gonna make me start pleading the blood of Jesus in here in a minute. Truth be told, I done already drenched my hands in that anointin' oil I got from Pastor last Sunday. Yep, made sure that I touched as much of that plane as I could as I was passing through the doorway and looking for a seat. Ain't no shame to my game. Probably need to rub some oil on that white lady as well. She looks like she needs some healing. Especially since she keep giving me the side-eye like I'm some leper or something.

It's OK though. 'Cause that right there is hurt in her eyes. I'd recognize it a mile away. And the worse kind of hurt at that. The kind that just rests on you. Like it's part of your make up and you don't have no way to shake it. No way to rid yourself of the thing that plagues you.
Now if there is one thing I know for sure, it's that pain don't discriminate. We're all broken. Now true, some of us have more cracks than others. Some of us, well, we just plain ole' in pieces. But we're all broken just the same. We all need Jesus for real. (Don't y'all make me shout on this plane!)

The truth is...folks are running around scared of each other and don't know why. Hate to say it but us church folks can be the worst. Looking on the outside, talking 'bout I go to a black church or white one. Now Lord knows I love me some good, food stomping, hand-clapping praise but I don't think I'd mind sitting and listening to some opera or country or whatever white folks listen to when they go to the church house. But that's just me. Most folks that call themselves children of God sittin' around judging folks on stuff that really don't matter in the long run. Sure ain't gonna matter in Heaven when we get our new bodies and stuff. Which reminds me. I need to talk to God about getting an advance copy of mine.

Now don't get me wrong. I'm not saying race don't matter. It does. Just not in the way that we think it does. See I'm a proud black woman. African American, as we call it now. Born in Birmingham, Alabama. When you look at me, I WANT you to see my baby smooth, blue-black skin; the soft, tight curls of my hair; the expanse of my nose and my hips. Especially that last one. I like to say I was made to breathe and birth...in the natural and the spiritual. (See there ya'll go again...makin' me shout!)

Go ahead and ask me why I pray the way I do, move the way I do, act the way I do. There's a story in it all and I'd be sure glad to share it with anyone willing to listen—white, brown, yellow, or green. Okay, maybe not green. I ain't talking to no green people.

Yep, got a great story to tell. But I suspect so does that white lady still sneaking peeks at me. Her eyes seem to be only a prologue to a tale I'd sure love to hear. But of course, that won't happen. 'Cause she scared. And if I'm honest, so am I. Might be for different reasons but I'm scared nonetheless.

So yeah, we'll sit here. Cups filled to the brim with word blessings just waiting to be received by the other and yet neither one of us willing to get to pouring. All because we've been taught some stupid concept called tolerance. Yes, I said it. Tolerance ain't worth a hill of beans! You tolerate a puppy peeing on your carpet. You celebrate human beings. I'm just sayin'.

Yeah, we'll probably end up doing just that: tolerating each other for the couple of hours or so we're on this plane and then going our separate ways.

But what will we miss, I wonder?

What kinds of revelations await us in the conversation we'll never have? The relationship we'll never explore. Well, we done already said so much with our eyes. Done exchanged pain and struggle and curiosity with just a glance or two. Shoot, this is nonsense! I need as many blessings I can get before I see Glory. And the way it looks...the way this plane is bouncing around the sky...glory might be coming sooner than I'd like.

"Excuse me, miss..."

6

The Problem With Forgiveness

Do some deaths have a purpose? I have to believe they do. Even the senseless ones. Even the deaths that are the result of evil or hate or mistrust or the ignorant reliance on and belief in stereotypes. Deaths like Philando Castille[1], Alton Sterling[2], Michael Brown, Eric Garner, Ezell Ford[3], Trayvon Martin, Renisha McBride[4], Oscar Grant[5], Sean Bell[6], Patric Dorismond [7], Amadou Diallo, Yusef Hawkins [8], Victor Steen[9], Ramarley Graham[10], Latasha Harlin[11], James Byrd Jr., Emmett Till and so on and so on.

Sadly, you can insert the latest name here:

_____

Death, unfortunately, can be a catalyst for change. So in that, there is purpose.
And if I believe change can come then, I suppose, so can reconciliation. And forgiveness. For all parties.

Whew! That's a hard pill to swallow.

This I know for sure: Compassion and forgiveness are the most necessary when it's the hardest to extend. I've seen this work itself out in the dark corners of my life. When I finally decided that those dark spaces within–the hurt and pain that resulted from other people's hurt and pain wielded against me–needed a little light, that light could only come from my own willingness to let some stuff go. So yes, I firmly believe that forgiveness is every instance is necessary because it has absolutely nothing to do with the person receiving it. It has everything to with the person giving it. It has everything to do with the person offering forgiveness not allowing the anger and frustration that can come from pain to rip them apart from the inside out.

But lately, I've also found this to be problematic.

Not forgiveness itself. As I said, I'm good with that. I have a problem with the way some people try to package it.

takes off halo

Sometimes I feel like screaming, or breaking something, or hitting someone when brown children and black men...people who look like my nephew, my brother, my baby girl, my hubby, me...can be shot and killed and some folks still have the audacity to give me the verbal equivalent of a pat on the head by telling me that I shouldn't speak out or protest or do anything about it because the "right thing to do" is to "turn the other cheek" or "forgive seventy times seven."

"There there now, Tracey. Don't you believe Jesus?"

Yes, I believe Jesus. I really do. But what do you tell people who have run out of cheeks to turn? When seventy times seven ran out centuries ago?

You say, "there's more to it."

Because there is.

Here's the thing: Forgiveness, and all the good it facilitates, is NOT the equivalent of blind allowance. Implying this is akin to suggesting that because Christ has forgiven us for our sin, we are not responsible for our actions afterward;

that there are no consequences and no need for grace and accountability. Most Christians would ever say that. And yet...

Forgiveness does not mandate that I be silent. Forgiveness does not mean neutrality. It doesn't mean that I shouldn't rally around those who are the victims of violence or demand justice from the same people I know I must forgive.

> "We do not talk about reconciliation until repair through reparations and accountability have been put in place. I'm not 'bearing with [allies] in love' if that phrase is simply a euphemism for my silence while a privileged person decides it hurts enough for them to act. I believe in partnership and coalition, but not on terms that maintain the comfort of those who are complicit in oppression." – Jasmine Banks, Writer and Activist

I get Jasmine. At some point, I have to think that a demand for compassion and forgiveness for those who hurt me or my children must somehow meet up with the demand for authentic repentance and justice. While a demand for peace is certainly right, every action has a reaction. There are consequences–some of which will be meted out by those being commanded to be peaceful. This is especially true in a world that increasingly refuses God and His grace.

Yep, there are definite consequences for evil and hate and mistrust and the ignorant reliance on and belief in stereotypes. Consequences that are evident in both the challenges within a community (for all of you "what about black on black crime?" folks) and the challenges externally.

And this unwillingness to even deal with, acknowledge, or *gasp* address both the root and the consequences of American racism (and any other ism for that matter) is the issue I have with many of those within my own faith who would rather just grab a scripture here or there or search their repertoire for religious platitudes in order to suggest that I (and other believers like me) should JUST forgive, pray and remain neutral when these "situations" come up.

You should forgive so shut up about it, they say.

Pray don't protest, they say.

He said he's sorry, they say.

You should forgive so don't call folks out when they wrong another human being, they say.

No. That's not how any of this works. Jesus was never neutral on the issues that mattered. Ever. (Ask the moneychangers in the temple that he drove out with whips).

I will forgive AND speak out, I say.

I will pray AND protest, I say.

I will forgive AND call folks out when they wrong another human being, I say. And here is the ironic thing about all of it: It is out of love and compassion that I MUST do the latter even as I'm doing the former. It's crazy to suggest that my compassion should kick in immediately when those who make the choice to kill a child is asked to be made accountable for that action BUT suggest that my compassion be placed on hold "until the investigation is complete" or "until all the facts are known" for the family who had to see their baby laying in the street for four hours. As the kids say, bad grammar and all, *"Where they do that at?"*

"Speak up for those who cannot speak for themselves, for the rights of all who are destitute. Speak up and judge fairly; defend the rights of the poor and needy." – Proverbs 31:8-9

Compassion should drive us all to pray for, speak out on behalf of, AND seek justice for those who are regularly–and in this case, very much REGULARLY–treated poorly by anyone...but particularly, a group who's sole purpose is supposed to be to protect and serve communities.

So umm yeah, if you are one of those church folk who are uncomfortable with the posts and shares of other believers on race and social justice, or whose silence on the matter has been DEAFENING, be as quiet about the issue as you like, pray as much as you want, but don't you dare conveniently use our faith as a justification for telling me to sit idly by as brown and black folks are treated less than human. Worse than dogs even. Doing that will make me model the righteous anger of my Savior for real and start turning up some tables and cracking some whips to drive out the thieves that are trying to sell that crock.

And be very clear: I am not violent nor an advocate for riots. Because I understand a thing, does not mean I think it is the best recourse. If a kid is hungry, hasn't eaten for days, and walks by a fruit stand and steals a banana, I certainly understand it. I don't have to condone stealing to say that I get WHY a person with such an UNMET NEED and such DESPERATION would resort to such a thing. I get why they wouldn't care about the consequences. As Dr. Martin

Luther King, Jr. once said and the previous chapter's title alludes to, "A riot is the language of the unheard."

I don't know about you but I hate when I'm not listened to. When Hubby zones out on me, I talk louder. When bosses in the past ignored me, I MADE my presence known. In hindsight, these were certainly not the best ways to establish my voice but it was what I resorted to in the moment of rage when I felt I had no other option.
And so goes Ferguson, MO. And Brooklyn, NY. And Los Angeles, CA. And if the long-standing, systemic problems of people of color are not acknowledged and addressed, a neighborhood near you. Because diversity comes with a cost even greater than discomfort. It comes with accountability. And differing views on how to enforce said accountability.

You know, I'll say this, though it may be a bit of tangent: I think a large segment of America, in general, loved the IDEA of having the first African American president. Folks of all races and backgrounds stood in voting lines for hours and came out in record numbers in 2008 and 2012. Afterward, we idealized what President Barack Obama's election meant with all our talk about post-racial this and the fulfillment of the dream that. But you know what? I don't think we were spiritually or psychologically ready for what his election would dredge up in our collective consciousness. Love him or hate him, we weren't ready. Then again, maybe I'm wrong. Maybe it was just the right time. Maybe it was time to rip off the tiny band aid we used to cover the gaping wound of racism. As I said, maybe there is a purpose in it all.

If there is any silver lining, it's this: these horrors can crack our hearts wide open if we let it. That's where I am right now. It's the ugly beautiful, I call it. That place that causes you great pain on one hand yet shows you just how capable you are of loving deeply and caring widely for those beyond your domain. For some, that means those who don't look like you. For most of us, it means those who don't affect your everyday life one iota. That kind of realization can be pretty amazing if you are willing to see it through.

In the meantime, hang on. I am.

---

[1] Philando Castile (1983-2016) was a 32 year-old African American man who was fatally shot by St. Paul, Minnesota police officer, Jeronimo Yanez during a traffic stop on July 6, 2016. Immediately following the shooting, Castile's girlfriend and passenger streamed the incident on Facebook Live. http://www.npr.org/sections/thetwo-way/2016/11/16/502314905/minn-police-officer-who-killed-philando-castile-is-charged-with-manslaughter

[2] Alton Sterling (1979-2016) was a 37 year-old African American man who was fatally shot while subdued by Baton Rouge police officers. Sterling's death was captured on video and went viral in July 2016. http://www.cnn.com/2016/07/07/us/baton-rouge-alton-sterling-shooting/

[3] Ezell Ford (1989-2014) was an African American man who suffered with mental illness. In August 2014, a LAPD officer shot Ford after he had been stopped in the Florence neighborhood. Ford's death sparked several protests and changes in LAPD protocol. http://www.latimes.com/local/lanow/la-me-ezell-ford-shooting-sg-storygallery.html

[4] Renisha McBride (1994-2013) was a 19 year-old African American teen that was fatally shot by a White homeowner in Dearborn Heights, Michigan on November 2, 2013 after her car crashed six blocks away. McBride was shot in the face and the shooter was found guilty of second-degree murder. http://michiganradio.org/post/what-really-happened-night-renisha-mcbride-died

[5] Oscar Grant III (1986-2009) was fatally shot in the back by Bay Area Rapid Transit (BART) police officer Johannes Mehserle on January 1, 2009 at the Fruitvale railway station. The ordeal was captured on cellphone video and subsequently made into the film, *Fruitvale Station*. https://www.theguardian.com/world/2010/jul/09/oscar-grant-oakland-police-shooting

6 Sean Bell (1983-2006) was a 23 year-old African American man who was fatally shot by New York City police officers on the night of his bachelor party. https://www.theguardian.com/world/2006/nov/27/usa.julianborger

7 Patrick Dorismond (1974-2000) was an African American security guard who was killed by undercover New York City police officers on March 16, 2000. http://www.cbsnews.com/news/no-trial-for-dorismond-shooter/

8 Yusef Hawkins (1973-1989) was an African American teen targeted by a group of White teens in the Bensonhurst section of Brooklyn, New York. The two men who led the group attack, Joseph Fama and Keith Mondello, were convicted of second-degree murder and minor charges, respectively. http://www.nydailynews.com/new-york/nyc-crime/yusef-hawkins-black-man-killed-white-mob-1989-article-1.2330613

9 Victor Steen (1991-2009) was a 17 year-old African American teen fatally struck by police car while riding his bike in Pensacola, Florida on October 3, 2009. The officer alleged he was attempting to question Steen after spotting him at a construction site. http://www.cnn.com/2009/CRIME/10/20/florida.boy.killed/

10 Ramarley Graham (1994-2012) was an 18 year-old teen that was fatally shot by New York City police officer, Richard Haste, in his grandmother's Bronx, NY apartment on February 2, 2012. Haste confronted Graham without serving a warrant. Graham's family settled with the New York City Police Department in 2015. http://www.huffingtonpost.com/2012/02/09/ramarley-graham-new-york-police- n 1266715.html

11 Latasha Harlins (1975-1991) was a 15 year-old African American teen that was fatally shot by a South Korean storeowner in South Central Los Angeles, CA after a dispute. Several months after the owner was sentenced, several Korean-owned businesses were targeted. http://articles.latimes.com/1997-02-11/local/me-27514 1 court-judge

7

Diary of a Protest

So I really wanted to go to DC or NYC for one of the marches for justice that were happening across the country that weekend. I'd actually been planning to go to DC all week long. But my daughter was sick (fever, snot, and such) and in a battle between my mommy-self and my activist-self, mommy usually wins. That's a truth I have yet to unpack. Anyway, in lieu of a trip to DC, I chose to participate in a protest in my own area in Philly. These were some of my chronicles of that experience:

2:05pm

So I'm headed to the protest. Sitting on the train at the 69th street EL/Subway station waiting to be shuttled to City Hall. I feel strange. A weird mix of anxiety and calm. I'm watching all these people on the platform. Black folks with bags. For some reason, I just see their bags and I know there's a metaphor in there somewhere. I suppose they've just gone Christmas shopping. Black and Brown folks with bags and backpacks and headphones. Carrying bags and not listening to anything out here. Yeah, there's definitely a metaphor in there. "Leave it alone, Imani!" A mom has just yelled at her girl child who keeps fiddling with a bag under the stroller. Been there before. There are white folks wandering around the platform. The same white folks I just saw in the station, trying to figure out how to use the token machine. They are obviously going to the protest. Had to be. I know it's wrong to make that generalization. Stereotype them. But they look lost. Like they've never been on the EL before but someone told them this was the best way to get to City Hall without the drama of parking and blocked streets. I mean, honestly, that's why I'm on the train. Lol. I don't know why that's funny to me. But I'm right, you know. The strawberry blonde just asked, "Is this the train to City Hall?" LOL. I told her yes. I guess I looked safe. I wonder why she didn't ask ole boy with the Beats by Dre headphones on and the sagging skinny jeans. Wait a minute...uhh yep, they are sagging skinny jeans. SMH.

2:17pm

The train is moving. Won't take long now. 46th street station. For non-Philly folks who will read this, I'm on a train that runs from Upper Darby (an alleged suburb right outside of the city) through West Philadelphia, a predominately African-American community that somehow magically diversifies around 40th street because of UPenn and Drexel. A mother and son are nearby. I'm staring at them but not weirdly or anything. Just in the way you can get away with on the subway. I can't help but to think of Michael Brown and his mom. Tamir Rice and his mom. Kind of clarifies things for me.

2:24pm

30th street station. The woman in front of me with deep gray locks and beautiful, brown skin is getting off. I'm disappointed. It's taking everything in me to not scream out, "No! Come back! It's just one more stop. You can stand with me. I'll stand with you." But I'm not going to do that. I don't know what she has to do today. I only know what I have to do. But I do wish that these were one and the same.

2:31pm

I don't see anyone. I'm standing on the north side of City hall and no one is here. Am I late? Was it only for a half hour? Impossible! No protest. No group. Nothing. I'm devastated. Do Black Lives Matter? I can't tell. Not yet. Maybe I'll wait. I want to cry.

As I waited to see if folks would show up, I took pictures of all the goings-on happening inside and outside of the City Hall courtyard. Folks ice skating, shopping, laughing, taking pictures by the big Christmas tree. Sure, I know life doesn't, shouldn't, better not stop because of what's happening. I understand that intellectually, even spiritually. But it's hard for my heart, my flesh to process this. And I found it very telling that in the place where there should have been thousands of people protesting injustice (see NYC and DC), there was...well, oblivion. That's how I saw it.

And then there was this: A high school chorus singing "I Had Christmas Down in Africa." The only two black girls in the group were dancing, arms linked, in front of the all-white chorus as a mostly white audience looked on.

Oblivion.

Like I said, I wanted to cry. The tears wouldn't come.

2:45pm

Okay found them. I was standing on the wrong side. That's it? That's all? 100, 150 people tops. 151 now.

2:55pm

We're walking silently around City Hall. Well, except for me speaking in my phone's audio recorder, there's silence. Many are holding up signs and placards that say, "Black Lives Matter" and "White Silence = Violence" and other quotes and phrases. Others, including me, are passing out these postcards that on one side have the name of an unarmed Black man or woman who was killed by police and, on the other side, has the details of their case. I had Oscar Grant.

3:01pm

We are walking through crowds of people who are laughing and ice skating, etc. You can feel the discomfort settling over them like a cloud. But I'm sad because that cloud seems to dissipate as soon as we pass—as though we were never there, as though our signs and placards are just a brief, tolerable annoyance. I want to cry. I feel impotent. As impotent as I felt sitting at home, behind my laptop, writing my article and blogs but wanting to do more.

We are such a small group (Observation: at least 60% of this group are white college students). The population of the metro Philly area is in the millions (and 40% African American).

3:11pm

We are still walking. We are being led slowly around the perimeter of the City Hall circle, weaving in and out of the courtyard, by a young brother—I believe he's a Temple student. He's wearing all white, with a list of all the murdered on his shirt. He has a mirror covering his face like a mask. I suppose he likes metaphors and symbolism too.

3:21pm

Someone, a curly-haired white guy, maybe Greek, has just suggested that we do a die-in[1] in the middle of the City Hall courtyard. "Fan out, let's take up as much of the space as possible," they are saying. I'm not sure how I feel about this. I want it to mean more. I guess I will settle for it meaning something. On the count of three...

As I laid on the ground, I watched the clouds move quickly across the sky. It felt like they were rushing. Like they too wanted to get out of there as fast as those tourists and shoppers did after we fell. I stared at the statue of an eagle that jutted out from the side of this 140 year old building. America's symbol of freedom and yet there I was, on the ground, asking for accountability, wondering if the seed of racism and white supremacy was planted too deep for people of color to ever truly be valued in this country. More than symbolism this time, it was irony, this eagle. One I couldn't ignore.

"Mommy, what are they doing?" small kids said.

"Thanks a lot for ruining my holiday," a woman's voice said.

150 people on the ground.

I was uncomfortable. I was cold. The subway rumbled underneath me. Several times I wanted to get up. Several times I wanted to say, "Are we done?" Then something shifted in me. I resisted my urge for comfort. So many of my ancestors endured dogs and water-hoses and lynchings—yet, they pressed on. Michael Brown laid in the street for four and half hours. He didn't get a chance to say, "Am I done? Is it over?" Eric Garner's last words were "I can't breathe!" so I dare not say "But I'm cold!"

My heart was heavy though. Because people walked pass and over us. Because of the Christmas music in the background. "All I want for Christmas..."

They see us, but they don't "see" us.

4:08pm

I'm on the train back to my car. It's packed on here. Blacks and Browns and Whites and others, going about their lives. In my haughtiness, in a moment of pseudo-righteousness, I want to judge them. I want to say, "Wake up!" I want to scream, "Don't you see?! There has to be more of us to make a difference!"

As soon as I thought this, something like emotional lightning struck my heart. It occurred to me that maybe I'd gotten it wrong. Maybe they weren't the ones who were asleep. Maybe they were the ones who were wide awake and I was asleep. They'd very clearly looked at the circumstance and decided on apathy and hopelessness. But I was still dreaming. Some of us are still dreaming. I want to say that the two hours I spent outside with those kids mattered. That, to a certain extent, just the idea of being out there (there goes that symbolism), will change one or two hearts. One or two hearts who will then change another one or two hearts and so on. Maybe they will pick up one of those postcards and read the name Oscar Grant or Jordan Baker or Tamir Rice and have a total shift in their thinking.

I keep talking about this heart thing because I think that's totally it. Until the hearts of people change, until there's a shift at the soul level, I don't know if authentic change can happen. You can legislate behavior but not beliefs.

Yet, I will try. If writing and protesting and "dying-in" can facilitate that happening, if these acts can be the vessels of awareness that God uses to allow that to happen, then it can't hurt to try. And because I know that "we wrestle not against flesh and blood but against principalities, against powers, against the rulers of the darkness of this world, against spiritual wickedness in high places," (Eph 6:12) I will continue to pray.

We must use ALL the weapons at our disposal.

---

[1] Die-in (n.): is a form of protest wherein participants simulate being dead. Also known as a lie-in. The Black Lives Matter Movement resurrected this form of protest in the wake of several deaths of African Americans at the hands of police across America.

https://www.washingtonpost.com/news/post-politics/wp/2015/01/21/black-lives-matter-protesters-stage-die-in-in-capitol-hill-cafeteria/

8

Blood at the Root

"Southern trees bear strange fruit
Blood on the leaves and blood at the root
Black bodies swinging in the southern breeze
Strange fruit hanging from the poplar trees"
- "Strange Fruit" by Billie Holiday

The terror that filled me made my heart race and stomach dance. Tears threatened to break free from my widened eyes. My hands shook as I took inventory of my situation. Full stop at stop sign. Check. Hands on the steering wheel at 10 and 2? Check. Seatbelt secure? Check. My preschooler strapped tightly into her car seat? Check. There was only one thing out of order.

One of my taillights was out.

I'd mentioned this to my husband a few days prior but, in the hustle and bustle of life, we just hadn't gotten around to fixing it. That happens, right? Of course it happens. But in that moment, as the blue lights of the cop car flashed behind me, I was acutely aware that other things happen also.

Sandra Bland[1] happened.

In that moment, a week or so after the Sandra Bland story hit, a couple of days after my 40th birthday, I was terribly clear that a broken taillight, a minor infraction, could turn into something else entirely. I understood that because I was in an area that didn't get many "like me" driving through it, any questions I might have about being stopped, any perceived tightness in my words or anger in my eyes, could very well lead to my death.

And even as the cop passed me and my breathing returned to its normal rate, I still gripped my steering wheel until my knuckles whitened. The "scare" had me so out of sorts that I pulled over to the side of the road to get myself together. After listening for a few seconds to my daughter, obliviously singing "Let it Go" from the Frozen soundtrack, I pulled back onto the road, as unsure as ever about how I could live free as a Black woman in this country; how I would teach my daughter how to be a Black girl in this country. How would I live in an environment where someone's perception of me as person of color—who I am, what I'm doing, why I'm doing it—could, perhaps, deceive them into believing that my death in the hands of those in authorities, no matter how sketchy the circumstances, *had* to be justified? How would I live in a place where my own perceptions of those in authority, those who have taken an oath to protect and serve me and my family would always—always—be tainted by the one too many instances where that authority was abused and that oath was broken?

And probably the saddest question I've had to ponder is this: How would I reconcile being part of a Christian community that, way too often, perceives these stories of injustice as overblown, isolated, lacking in "critical" information, and ultimately, not worthy of any action or stand?

It's not okay for an unarmed person to die in police custody. Angry words, though powerful, though sometimes even subject to consequences, are never a license to kill.

I know, I know. Sandra Bland's death was ruled a suicide.

Although there are still many unanswered questions about the circumstance of her death——I'm willing to concede the *possibility* that she killed herself. PTSD is real. Just as real as a subdural hematoma.

I'm also very willing to say that the unnecessary but all too common actions of Officer Brian Encina *led* to her killing herself. I'm even more willing to say that the possibility of Officer Encina having unfounded perceptions of Sandra Bland—perceptions formed by stereotypes and generalizations—could have deceived him into thinking that it was somehow okay to treat someone violating a minor traffic law, someone not unlike myself with the broken tail light, with such force and aggression as he did when he yanked this woman out of her car and slammed her onto the ground. His actions, and Sandra's perception that she actually had certain rights as a driver—namely to question the requests of the officer—led to her death as well.

"If she had only cooperated with the cop, she wouldn't have been arrested."

First, cooperation and complicity doesn't guarantee safety. Ask Philando Castile.

Secondly, a part of me knows where this thinking comes from. As humans, we want a reason for horrible things happening. We desire truth and facts and specifics because it helps us place these awful injustices in boxes that we can see, feel, and understand. The same goes for those who say, *"there's not enough information available about what happened."* For some, the evidence of injustice alone is not enough. Even video of the aggressive actions of a cop are not enough. We need a reason. Some White Christians, those who would be potential allies in movements against injustice, often need to be absolutely sure there's enough reason to stand up for some reason. They need perfect victims. They need to know that there's nothing nefarious about the victim—marijuana in the system, stealing cigarellos, owing child support—that would make *them* look bad. Sadly, a woman getting her head smashed into the ground by a police officer for not putting out her cigarette is just not enough information.

Borrowing from the Billie Holiday song, *Strange Fruit*, there's certainly some "blood at the root" of this thing, for sure.

I wonder what would have happened if Jesus needed more information about the woman caught in adultery before standing between her and the stones held by men prepared to put her to death. What if He said, "I can't defend her yet. All the facts aren't out."

Oh to be more like Him.

Plus, I'm not sure that Sandra's cooperation would have made a difference. It's possible, sure. But it's equally possible that the deeply held stereotypes Bland, in biased eyes, fit—that she was just another Black person up to no good; that her questioning of authority was indicative of the typical angry Black woman and needed to be put in check—had taken root in the mind and heart of the officer. The truth is, there have been numerous cases where cooperation—whether it's having one's hands up in a posture of surrender or answering questions—has not rendered a different outcome as hers. Sandra, a voice in the online #BlackLivesMatter movement, knew that too.

Let's dump the respectability argument once and for all.

I think it's way too easy for those in denial about the deep racial wounds that exist in our country and the threads of white supremacy woven in our justice system and dare I say, in the Church, to believe that cooperation from victims in these cases is somehow more significant than accountability and restraint and the following of procedures from officers who abuse their authority. This is not surprising, I suppose. It was the same narrative played out with Jesus. What happened to Christ in the custody of authorities prior to His crucifixion, some would argue, was also a result of His lack of cooperation. Questioned by the Sanhedrin, brought before King Herod and Pontius Pilate, Jesus chose the authority given to him by God over the authority given to these men. He knew His rights.

I hear you super-saved, church folk out there: How dare you compare this woman to Jesus?

Robin Caldwell, a PR professional and a sorority sister of Bland gave me some insight on this: "[Sandra] was a believer. A lifelong AME. Her family [was filled] with strong women of faith. She was edgy—so am I—but she believed. The bible says 'render under Caesar what's Caesar's and God's to God.' In some way, I'd like to think that she was a good steward over her earthly citizenship because she questioned the arrest. She asked questions. She didn't submit blindly to authority."

And ultimately, whether from suicide or murder, she died because of that.

As, I believe, Jesus did for all for us.

So maybe, just maybe that's Sandra's legacy. And the legacy of women like Natasha McKenna[2], Tanisha Anderson[3], Yvette Smith[4] and many others who have died suspiciously in police custody. Maybe their deaths will make so much noise, create so much change, that their bodies will stand in the place of mine. Or my mother's. Or my *Frozen*-loving daughter's.

Lord, I hope so.

---

[1] Sandra Bland (1987-2015) was a 28 year-old African American woman who was found hanged in a jail cell in Waller County, Texas after her arrest on July 10, 2015. The controversy surrounding Bland's death inspired the Twitter hash tag #sayhername
https://www.thenation.com/article/what-happened-to-sandra-bland/

[2] Natasha McKenna (1978-2015) was an African American woman who died while restrained in police custody in Fairfax, Virginia on February 8, 2015. McKenna was handcuffed, placed in leg shackles, had a spit mask placed over her head, and was tasered as police attempted to transport her. She was pronounced dead after suffering cardiac arrest and losing consciousness.
https://www.washingtonpost.com/local/crime/death-of-woman-shocked-by-stun-gun-in-fairfax-jail-is-ruled-an-accident/2015/04/28/7bc85f36-edfc-11e4-a55f-38924fca94f9_story.html

[3] Tanisha Anderson (1978? -2015) was an African American woman who died in Cleveland Police custody after being placed in the 'prone position' by an officer. Anderson lived with bipolar disorder and heart disease; medical professionals ruled these conditions may have increased her likelihood of sudden death.
http://www.cleveland.com/metro/index.ssf/2015/01/tanisha_anderson_was_restraine.html

[4] Yvette Smith (1967? -2014) was a 47 year-old African American who was fatally shot by Bastrop County (Texas) Sheriff's Deputy, Daniel Willis, as he attempted to respond to a 911 call. Smith was unarmed.
http://kxan.com/2014/03/12/autopsy-report-indicates-yvette-smith-was-shot-twice-by-deputy/

9

The Hope of a New Movement

We all have heard the stories. They usually begin with "back in my day..." and what follows is a litany of exaggerated narratives about how life back then was so much harder than the present. How she— usually some gray-haired elder wearing a pillbox hat and compression stockings, hiding the tobacco chilling between her gums and teeth—don't know why us young folk are so ungrateful.

"Back in my day, I had to walk five miles to school, barefoot, in the snow, carrying ten books, a box of pencils and a lunch pail."

"Back in my day, we didn't have none of this new fangled text messaging. If we wanted to send someone a message we had to write a letter and walk five miles to the post office, barefoot, in the snow, carrying ten books, a box of pencils and a lunch pail."

Sure you did.

I always found it amazing that they could simultaneously talk about how different things were, how much had changed, while also claiming that there was "nothing new under the sun." Every dance, style, way of being, harkens back to days of old, according to my Granny. Or "you all think Ferguson is something," some of my elders back home will say. "I remember when King came to Kentucky to march in Frankfort for civil rights."

Ain't nothing new under the sun, they say.

Some of their stories were more sobering though. They shared with us the struggles endured in the Jim Crow south or, for those who were part of the Great Migration that Isabel Wilkerson talks about in her book *The Warmth of Other Suns*, the many hardships and trials that came from trying to make a better life in the North. I suppose both the ridiculousness and soberness of all these stories, the alleged contradictions between new and old, was kind of a way to illustrate the tension between the past and present.

As a card-carrying member of Generation X, I suppose I will be doing the same in a few years, linking the past with the present. Maybe even sooner.

I remember going to see the film SELMA during its opening weekend here in Philadelphia. It was a brilliant film that held me captive from start to finish with its amazing images, powerful words, and dynamic acting. But what I was most taken with, what caught me most off guard, was the familiarity of the film. I felt like I'd been there. Strange since I was born a decade after Bloody Sunday[1].

After some reflection, I finally realize why I felt so connected to the story. I now know why watching a police officer walk up to Dr. King and punch him in the mouth for no reason caused the hair on my arms to stand at attention. It's because even in my lifetime I've seen unarmed black men regularly treated with the same disregard. Abused, sometimes killed, for no other reason than they "fit the description."

Ain't nothing new under the sun, they say.

It hurt to sit in that theater and realize that what I was seeing on the screen was not just some depiction or interpretation of a long-gone historical event, but at its core, a present reality. That the thread of white supremacy remains deeply embedded in the fabric of our institutions—despite the many sacrifices of our mothers and fathers.

It also hurts to look at your child and realize that 40 years from now, if true change doesn't somehow find its way to the hearts and minds of some, she could be sitting in a movie theater watching a film called Ferguson or Staten Island and sensing the same familiarity her mother does today.

Yet in spite of this tension I feel, this convergence of past and present, I still have hope. A crazy, seemingly unfounded, hope. My hope means that maybe, just maybe history will not repeat itself; that we can somehow make room in our world for more love instead of hate.

Sure, on many days, I think my hope is futile. Even foolish. But then I remember this:
And let us not grow weary while doing good, for in due season we shall reap if we do not lose heart. – Galatians 6:9 NKJV

Hope is my good. I cannot grow weary of having hope even when it's exhausting to do so. Our mothers and father in Selma (and Montgomery and Frankfort and…) didn't stop hoping. Hope fueled their courage. It will fuel my own.

And maybe when daughter is my age, with her own children, I can pull up on my compression socks, straighten my pillbox hat, and talk about what happened "back in my day" and how "these kids got it easy these days with all their equality, justice, and thangs."

Maybe there *can* be something new under the sun.

---

[1] Bloody Sunday (March 7, 1965) occurred when members of the Student Nonviolent Coordinating Committee (SNCC), along with Martin Luther King Jr., the Southern Christian Leadership Conference (SCLC) and six hundred marchers were met with police violence as they attempted to cross the Edmund Pettus Bridge in Selma, Alabama.
http://www.usatoday.com/story/news/nation/2015/03/05/black-history-bloody-sunday-timeline/24463923/

10

A Fight in Two Realms

For we wrestle not against flesh and blood, but against principalities, against powers, against the rulers of the darkness of this world, against spiritual wickedness in high places. – Ephesians 6:12

The stories of my enslaved ancestors resonate with me for numerous reasons. Many of which are spiritual. I think it's the idea of being bound and then free. The last time I remember being truly free was when I was three years old. At three, my mind and heart was pure. My spirit was alive with the possibilities of life. I knew nothing of bondage.

Then, seemingly out of nowhere, the enemy of my soul, the worst of all slave masters, used the trials of life and the manipulation of those who were supposed to love and protect me, to snatch away my peace. I was handed pounds and pounds of fear and told me to carry it or else. This counterfeit enslaved me with the weight of the sins that were made against me and later, my own.

And you know what?

After a while, feeling helpless and unable to fight, I accepted my fate. I lived in bondage and tried to "make do."

But my heart remembered. My soul remembered what it was like to be free in spirit. And it longed for that time.

"I don't want to survive. I want to live."
– Solomon Northrup in the book and film, Twelve Years a
Slave

For 25 of my 41 years on this earth, I settled on survival. As good as any "slave" I could keep my head down and smile like everything was alright. I went to church, I read my bible, but I struggled with allowing the spirit of God to live completely in my heart, to trust that the blood of Jesus had set me free from all the pain, heartache and even the unforgiveness I harbored in my heart. The scars on my spiritual back were the result of the whipping I'd received by life and living; wounds that seemed to re-open in every relationship I had and many of the choices I made.

Ten years ago, I began the long road back to spiritual freedom. If I'm honest, I'll say that I'm not there yet. Every step I take is arduous. There are moments when I feel like I've been recaptured and sent back to the field. But just like my ancestors before me, I will never forget who I really am. I am a child of God. Meant to live free in Him.

And just like in my social justice work, I will take the risk to tell that to anyone I can.

11

The Possibility of
(and Biblical Precedence for) Revolt

I consider myself a peaceful person. For me, this simply means that I don't believe that most problems can be solved through violence or aggression. I've lived most of my life by the mantra that says, "conflict is inevitable but combat is optional." I don't avoid confrontations but I certainly don't take up arms every time I'm confronted. Now this does not mean I don't get angry. Of course I get angry. As an empathic person who's constantly learning how to manage my hypersensitivity, I can get extremely...umm...passionate about things.

removes halo

There have even been times in my life when I've been so enraged that punching someone in the throat has totally felt like a completely reasonable action.

But I usually make another choice.

Yet as I sat and watched my social media newsfeed explode with comments about the release of another video showing an unarmed and innocent Black man—Terence Crutcher—being shot down in the street by the police—this only days after 13 year old Tyre King was shot in the back for "playing while black"—I was also very clear that for many, the only response to such state sanctioned violence against black people (state sanctioned because in a large percentage of these cases, officers are not held accountable) was ultimately going to be one of revolt.

And as scary as that is, as much as I hope for another alternative, I get it.

See, both the perpetrators and beneficiaries of systemic racism are not invested in seeing change. Even allies, though necessary in most freedom movements, often have limits to how much they are willing to risk to see systems overhauled. This is because their power and privileges are deeply embedded in the status quo. The oppression of people of color is as American as grid-iron football. You know, physical and psychological violence that's widely accepted and cheered on from the stands. Sounds like our political rallies of late.

How long do you think any group will stand by and watch their husbands and wives, mothers and fathers, their children killed in the street; their deaths looped on media like some modern-day gladiator exhibition, before an uprising is contemplated? Until defending your family, property, and livelihoods by any means necessary becomes a reality?
Well, what about the Civil Rights movement? Black people accomplished so much without violence back then, Tracey.

Yes, they did. And I understand why even some Black folks like to sit back on their respectable haunches and say, "just march and protest more. Don't riot. Don't fight back." Many come from an era and movement where non-violent protest was ONE particular strategy used to gain rights for Black people. They see their work as a being successful and, if implemented strategically now, still potentially useful. And I don't necessarily disagree. But it's important to understand that non-violence was one of MANY strategies during the movement. Whether we want to admit it or not, the Black Panther Party and other movements whose focus were on empowerment and self-defense were very influential. Otherwise why would Hoover and the rest of our government at the time be so hell bent on stopping them?

Secondly, and probably most important to note, America has tried everything possible to ensure that the unity among black people that existed during the 50s and 60s never happens again. The one-mindedness among people of color that made the Civil Rights movement even possible has been systematically dismantled through the insidious infiltration of drugs into our communities in the 70s and 80s—resulting in even more insidious breaking up of families, reminiscent of slavery—bussing and other pseudo-integration efforts. Yes, laws were changed. And some of us made it out of the hood. Some of us even made it to the White House. But many of us, in an effort to succeed, were forced to do so through assimilation. In way too many cases, we had to sacrifice anything that remotely connected us to our culture in order to achieve the "American Dream" and become "the good Negro." That gap makes unifying under one common cause challenging. Oh you didn't know? Black folks too can be perpetuators and enablers of white supremacy and the status quo.

I've said it before and I'll say it again: Between the foolery that is our current election, the almost daily onslaught of what I call "Black death porn" by the media—the desensitizing of an audience to violence against people of color (Ask yourself when you've seen a white person blown away on the news?)—we are nearing that I mentioned earlier. That "moment when an idea, trend, or social behavior crosses a threshold, tips, and spreads like wildfire." We are nearing the point where the idea of revolt is becoming less implausible to more and more people.

People who are simply tired of seeing another hashtag with another man, woman, or child's name on it.

But Black folks should just sit back and somehow continuously accept the continued devaluing of our very humanity, right? Langston Hughes best captured the feeling I'm sensing nowadays, in his poem, *Warning.*

Negroes,
Sweet and docile,
Meek, humble and kind:
Beware the day
They change their mind!
Wind
In the cotton fields,
Gentle Breeze:
Beware the hour
It uproots trees!

And before the saints get all flustered, countering with platitudes about Jesus and love and peace, let's be 100% clear about what the Bible says. Yes, Jesus is about redemptive love. He IS redemptive love. Yes, Jesus tells us to love our enemies. Yes, Jesus says forgive 70 x 7. Yes, Jesus said that if one takes up the sword, he or she will die by the sword (the cost of war). Jesus clearly states to turn the other cheek at an INDIVIDUAL offense. But He also says shake the dust off your feet and leave a place where you are clearly not welcomed (Matthew 10:14). He also clearly advocates for the protection and defense of the marginalized and disenfranchised. Scripture outlines the role of those who believe to be defenders of those who are oppressed. (see: Matt. 19:21, Luke 4:18-19, Levi. 19:15, Proverbs 31:8-9) So let's be a bit more nuanced when cherry picking our scriptures, 'kay?

Here's another truth: Justice/Freedom, and the sometimes violent fight for either, is not a foreign concept in scripture. Sure, God does not want war. But he has clearly allowed it to occur—especially in the defense of righteousness. There were times where God called Israel to defend themselves in battle. Mostly because mankind, with its free will and all, had already created a culture of war and bloodshed. When the Midianites cut off important resources to Israel, God raised up Gideon to fight them—not as aggressors but in defense of their families and property.

So how much more should a reasonable person expect from a group that has experienced...

- 250 years of enslavement which, in case you didn't know, included the breaking up of families, the rape and slaughter of women, men and children, the beating and whipping of HUMANS, the building of this nation through unpaid labor
- 100+ years of jim Crow, segregation, lynching, and under-education of their youth
- 50+ years of redlining, inequities in education, mass incarceration, media stereotyping and framing, police brutality and profiling, cultural appropriation and pillaging, etc.

Very few groups in the world have had such heinous acts committed against them and not responded in kind for their freedom. Haiti fought the French (enslavers/colonizers) for independence and there are numerous national liberation movements that have occurred over oh, the last few centuries. Google it.
America itself has fought entire wars for lesser ideals (see: Vietnam, Iraq, etc). In fact, it's been very clear over the last two decades that our country is not going to allow so-called Islamic extremists to repeatedly attempt to or succeed in

blowing up or killing Americans without some aggressive response.

So there it is. For many African Americans, hope is walking a tightrope in this circus called a democracy. And every Black body in the street, every acquittal of a White murderer, every obvious disparity in our justice, education, and economic systems is like a rushing wind ready to knock the little hope we have left into the sea of our other losses.

And you know what happens when one feels as though there is nothing left to lose, right?

Without a true systemic overhaul—an absolute yanking up by the root the weeds of white supremacy planted as seeds at the inception of this country—happening alongside a spiritual overhaul of the hearts and minds of those who either deny that black lives don't matter nowadays or actually believe that they don't—a revolt by people of color who are hopeless and fed up will be inevitable.

And dare I say it...justified.

God help us all.

12

Privilege Exists

I could tell she felt awkward. Concern was written all over her face. Her pale skin had turned slightly pink. Her eyebrows were furrowed. Her words were clear but filled with emotion.

"This feels awkward. And a little unfair."

He, on the other hand, was totally relaxed. Hands in his pockets. Expressionless. A couple of shrugs and these words: "I'm a straight, white male. I kind of knew this would happen."

Both were standing in front of the class, a significant distance from the rest of their peers who were spread out across the room, in various positions, front to back. They were all students in one of my English courses who'd just participated in our class privilege walk exercise. I'd gotten the idea from a recent video experiment conducted by Buzzfeed and wanted to use it to illustrate some of the ideas put forth in one of the articles we were reading: Peggy McIntosh's *White Privilege[1]: Unpacking the Invisible Knapsack*. The privilege walk exercise works like this: students are asked to stand in a straight line across one side of the room. As I ask specific questions related to race, class, gender, sexual orientation, they move forward or backward depending on their answer. The point is to use a visual to drive home the validity and complexities of privilege, in general, and white privilege, specifically.

Some of my white students, like the young man I mentioned earlier, totally got it. They were pretty clear that they experience privilege daily because of the color of their skin. The young woman who ended up in the front of the privilege walk was even able to recount a time when she and a friend, also white, were walking down the street with two Black men and confronted by police. The two white girls were immediately let go. The two Black men were taken downtown where they spent the weekend in custody. "For no reason," she said with a slight sadness. Her story caused one of the Black women in the class, who'd landed somewhere in the middle of the pack, to turn her head as tears filled her eyes. The exercise was truly illuminating for all of them.

However, there were other students in the class who were less willing to accept the notion that they were somehow privileged because they were white. "I'm not privileged because I'm white. I've had a very rough life. We were poor. We struggled," one student announced.

There it is.

My student's defensiveness is all too common. In a study conducted by L. Taylor Phillips and Brian S. Lowery for the *Journal of Experimental Social Psychology*, the denial of racial privilege is significant among policy makers and power brokers. This inability (or refusal) to see privilege, of course, leads to a lack of consideration or action when it comes to issues related to racism. Think about it: If you don't believe that inequality exists, you are not likely to fight for the dismantling of systems that others tell you promote it. Phillips and Lowery note that acknowledging racial privilege "may be difficult given that Whites are motivated to believe that meritocratic systems and personal virtues determine life outcomes... however, claiming personal life hardships may help Whites manage the threatening possibility that they benefit from privilege."

This is likely why so many of my students – black and white – were visibly moved by the privilege walk. The exercise demonstrated clearly those who benefited from privilege—as well as those who didn't (see the transgender man who was in the back of the class by the end of the exercise).

No one sees their privilege from their position in life. Their lens is tainted by circumstances and personal experience. But the truth is, privilege really isn't about what *you* recognize or what *you* see. It's about what *others* see in you. It's about how you are perceived based on the color of your skin and how those perceptions afford you benefits that others don't receive. So take note: just because you don't see your privilege doesn't mean it isn't there or that you don't benefit from it.

Much of the "but I had it bad too" defense from those who are challenged on their racial privilege is rooted in this notion that somehow if you are white and poor or white and come from a tragic home environment that exists because you are poor, then you have somehow bypassed your white privilege. But conflating racial privilege with class privilege just doesn't work when compared to the actual facts: According to Maryhelen MacInnes, Hsin-Yi Liu, Jana Knibb and Leslie Killgore in an article for *The Providence Journal*, "When class is held constant, race remains a factor in negative health outcomes for African-Americans. Class advantage also does not protect minorities against bearing the brunt of environmental racism and the accompanying health risks." Studies have found that environmental zoning and protection laws are enforced unequally across states, counties and neighborhoods, leaving communities of color, regardless of their socioeconomic status, in the position of being vulnerable to highly polluted environments.

But I gather that the defensiveness of some white people comes from the fear of being categorized as racist if they acknowledge their racial privilege. Let me help you with that: It doesn't make you racist that you have privilege. Barring extreme efforts, you can't change your skin nor how people perceive it. I'm not even inclined to tell you to turn down your benefits (provided that there isn't an obvious transgression against a person of color a la my student's white girls go free story). However, you just might be racist though if you continue to deny the existence of white privilege with the intention to somehow neutralize the voracity in which people of color express and demonstrate how that privilege and the white supremacist system that supports it impacts us. Why? Because the only reason anyone would deny what has been obviously documented over the last century would be because either consciously or unconsciously they have a desire to maintain their status. By vanquishing the complaints, you keep your benefits. By acknowledging the complaints and aligning with the complainants, you essentially are saying that you want to sacrifice the benefits afforded to you based on skin color alone in order for everyone to be treated equally.

But no worries. That's not likely to happen. White privilege is the favorite child of White Supremacy and has to be dismantled at both the heart level and in our systems simultaneously. Even if prison, education, and economic systems were righted, we would still have to contend with "the hearts of men." And that's a much more challenging battle. I'd go as far as to say an impossible one. So as long as there are employers who still see a white man in a suit with an impeccable resume but maybe a tragic, impoverished past as still smarter, more intelligent, more qualified than a Black or Brown man with all the same attributes, your white privilege, denied or acknowledged, is safe.

So why acknowledge it then? Well, because acknowledging it and aligning yourself with those who are fighting for social equality and justice is a step toward change. Because, make no mistake, righting the wrongs of our white supremacist systems is still all too necessary. In fact, doing so becomes even more critical simply *because* of the impossibility of human beings' ability to change other human beings' hearts. Dismantling systems means that if that employer who hires according to his racist heart gets caught, he will be held accountable by a justice system that is truly blind—and not just wearing cool shades like the one we have today. It means that elected officials who are called on the carpet for their racist comments will have to wrestle with the fear of losing their jobs or the support of their constituency as opposed to simply riding out the tumultuous waves of our 24-hour social media news cycle. It means that Officer Daniel Panteleo could have choked out Eric Garner or those deputies could have tased Natasha McKenna to death or George Zimmerman still might have killed Trayvon Martin, but all of them would be rotting away in jail right now.

So now you know. White privilege exists. And white people benefit from it regardless of any other status held (class, gender, etc.). Ironically, it is this same white privilege that gives white people the agency to either deny or acknowledge it. But in the words of that prophetic voice from hip-hop's golden age, Black Sheep, "The choice is yours."

Choose wisely.

*(This essay was originally published at
www.forharriet.com)*

---

[1] Peggy McIntosh is a White American feminist and social justice advocate. Her work promotes racial, sexual, gender equity in schools, industry, and society. Her seminal text, "White Privilege: Unpacking the Invisible Knapsack" (1989) deconstructs whiteness and the preeminence the category has in American culture.
http://www.newyorker.com/books/page-turner/the-origins-of-privilege
http://code.ucsd.edu/~pcosman/Backpack.pdf

Recommended Reading and Other Sources

Please note that some of these sources are secular. As the experiences of Black people in America is not a monolithic one, I think it's absolutely critical for white people, white Christians in particular, to familiarize themselves with the diversity of our historical and cultural experiences. Though some of these texts and authors are not Christian, there is still value in the scholarship as well as the lived experiences represented here. As my great-grandmother used to say, "Eat the meat, spit out the bones."

Books

Morrison, Toni
Playing in the Dark: Whiteness and the Literary Imagination
Harvard University Press
1992

Degruy, Joy
Post Traumatic Slave Syndrome
Uptone Press
2005

DuBois, W.E.B.
The Souls of Black Folk: Essays and Sketches
A.C McClure & Co.
1903

Cleveland, Christena
Disunity in Christ: Uncovering the Hidden Forces that Keep Us Apart
IVP
2013

DeYoung, Curtiss Paul
Boesak, Allen
Radical Reconciliation: Beyond Political Pietism and Christian Quietism
Orbis
2012

McNeil, Brenda Salter
Roadmap to Reconciliation
InterVarsity
2016

Tatum, Beverly Daniel
"Why Are All the Black Kids Sitting Together in the Cafeteria?" And Other Conversations About Race
Hachette
2003

Rah, Soong-Chan
Prophetic Lament - A Call for Justice in Troubled Times
IVP
2015

Friere, Paulo
Pedagogy of the Oppressed
Originally translated into English, 1970
Several editions since then.

Shakur, Assata
Assata: An Autobiography
Lawrence Hill Books
1987

Alexander, Michelle
The New Jim Crow: Mass Incarceration in the Age of Colorblindness
The New Press
2012

Coates, Ta'Nehisi
Between the World and Me
Spiegel & Grau
2015
Baldwin, James
The Fire Next Time
Vintage
1992

Laymon, Kiese
How to Slowly Kill Yourself and Others in America
Agate Bolden
2013

Davis, Angela Y.
Freedom is a Constant Struggle
Haymarket Books
2016

Haley, Alex
Roots: The Sage of an American Family
Da Capo Press
1976; 2016

West, Cornel
Race Matters
Vintage
1994

Woodson, Carter G.
The Miseducation of the Negro
Tribeca Books
1933; 2013

hooks, bell
killing rage: Ending Racism
Holt Paperbacks
1996
Zinn, Howard
A Peoples' History of the United States
Harper Perennial Modern Classics
2015

Hill, Marc Lamont
Nobody: Casualties of America's War on the Vulnerable from Ferguson to Flint and Beyond
Atria Books
2016

Fanon, Frantz
The Wretched of the Earth
Grove Press
2005

Wright, Richard
Black Boy
Harper Perennial Modern Classics
1945

Angelou, Maya
I Know Why the Caged Bird Sings
Ballantine Books
1969

Burrell, Tom
Brainwashed: Challenging the Myth of Black Inferiority
SmileyBooks
2010

Wilkerson, Isabel
The Warmth of Other Suns: The Epic Story of America's Great Migration
Vintage
2011

Jacobs, Harriet
Incidents in the Life of a Slave Girl
Thayer & Eldridge
1861

McCall, Nathan
Makes Me Want to Holler: A Young Black Man in America
Random House
1994

Truth, Sojourner
Narrative of Sojourner Truth
Dover Thrift Editions
1850

Gates, Henry Louis
Thirteen Ways of Looking at a Black Man
Vintage
1997

Collins, Patricia Hill
From Black Power to Hip Hop: Racism, Nationalisn, and Feminism
Temple University Press
2006

Douglass, Frederick
Narrative of the Life of Frederick Douglass
Dover Publications
1845

Douglas, Kelly Brown
Stand Your Groud: Black Bodies and the Justice of God
Orbis Books
2015

Dyson, Michael Eric
Come Hell or High Water: Hurricane Katrina and the Color of Disaster
Basic Civitas Books
2006

Harris-Perry, Melissa
Sister Citizen: Shame, Stereotypes, and Black Women in America
Yale University Press
2011

Shapiro, Thomas
The Hidden Cost of Being African American: How Wealth Perpetuates Inequality
Oxford University Press
2003

Jordan, June
Some of Us Did Not Die: New and Selected Essays
Basic Civitas Books
2002

Smith, Mycal Denzel
Invisible Man, Got the Whole World Watching: A Young Black Man's Education
Nation Books
2016

Thurston, Baratunde
How to Be Black
Harper Paperbacks
2012

Marable, Manning
Let Nobody Turn Us Around: Voices on Resistance, Reform, and Renewal: An African American Anthology
Rowman & Littlefield Publishers
1999

Gates, Henry Louis
Life Upon These Shores: Looking at African American History, 1513-2008
Knopf
2013

Painter, Nell Irvin
Creating Black Americans: African-American History and Its Meanings, 1619 to the Present
Oxford University Press
2006

Kivel, Paul
Uprooting Racism: How White People Can Work for Racial Justice
New Society Publishers
2011

Lester, Julius
Let's Talk About Race
Amistad
2008

Bonilla-Silva, Eduardo
Racism without Racists: Color-Blind Racism and the Persistence of Racial Inequality in America
Rowman & Littlefield Publishers
2013

Lopez, Ian Haney
Dog Whistle Politics: How Coded Racial Appeals Have Reinvented Racism and Wrecked the Middle Class
Oxford University Press
2015

Smith, Chip
The Cost of Privilege: Taking on the System of White Supremacy and Racism
Camino Press
2007

Rothenberg, Paula
White Privilege: Essential Readings on the Other Side of Racism
Worth Publishers
2015

Joseph, Peniel
Waiting 'Til the Midnight Hour: A Narrative of Black Power in America
Holt Paperbacks
2007

Haley, Alex
The Autobiography of Malcolm X
Ballantine Books
1965

Carson, Clayborne
The Autobiography of Martin Luther King Jr.
Warner Books
2001

Washington, Booker T.
Up From Slavery
Dover Thrift Editions
1901

Kendi, Ibram
Stamped From the Beginning: The Definitive History of Racist Ideas in America
Nation Books
2016

Television and Film

13th: From Slave to Criminal with One Amendment
Directed by Ava Duverney for Netflix Films

The Central Park Five
Directed by Ken Burns
The African Americans: Many Rivers to Cross
Hosted by Henry Louis Gates for PBS

Dark Girls
Produced by D. Channsin Berry and Bill Duke

Articles and other resources

Syllabus for White People to Educate Themselves
https://docs.google.com/document/d/1By9bUjJ78snEeZuLXN
GBdlVMJgEQWMEjR-
Gfx8ER7Iw/mobilebasic#heading=h.bi12zdslqy3z

Channing, Austin
Conversations, Deflections and Responses. A free downloadable guide
https://static1.squarespace.com/static/50e26f21e4b0c2f497
6dc211/t/559331b9e4b08369d0220182/1435709881326/8
+Conversation+Deflections-2.pdf

Yates, Ashley
Millenial Activist Ashley Yates: "Voting Can Help End Police Brutality. No, I'm Not Joking"
ColorLines Magazine
http://www.colorlines.com/articles/millennial-activist-ashley-yates-voting-can-help-end-police-brutality-no-im-not-joking
Nov-16

King, Shaun
Solutions for police brutality can begin with our overwhelmingly white male justice system
NY Daily News
http://www.nydailynews.com/news/national/king-police-brutality-fix-change-systems-racial-makeup-article-1.2725465
1-Jul-16

Smith, Jack
To stop police brutality, we must end the epidemic of PTSD among officers
Mic Magazine https://mic.com/articles/154241/to-stop-police-brutality-we-must-end-the-epidemic-of-ptsd-among-officers#.yp0PhHaKF
Sep-16

Danticat, Edwidge
Enough is Enough
The New Yorker
http://www.newyorker.com/culture/cultural-comment/michael-brown-ferguson-abner-louima-police-brutality
Nov-14

Huckabee, Tyler
The Problem with Saying 'All Lives Matter'
Relevant Magazine
http://www.relevantmagazine.com/current/nation/problem-saying-all-lives-matter
Jul-15

Garza, Alicia
The Creation of A Movement
Black Lives Matter Website
http://blacklivesmatter.com/herstory/

Cobb, Jelani
The Matter of Black Lives
The New Yorker
http://www.newyorker.com/magazine/2016/03/14/where-is-black-lives-matter-headed
Mar-16

Funes, Yessenia
WATCH: Standing Rock Documentary Sheds Light on #NoDAPL Fight
ColorLines Magazine -
http://www.colorlines.com/articles/watch-standing-rock-documentary-sheds-light-nodapl-fight
Nov-16

Avins, Jenni
The Dos and Don'ts of Cultural Appropriation
The Atlantic
http://www.theatlantic.com/entertainment/archive/2015/10/the-dos-and-donts-of-cultural-appropriation/411292/
Oct-15

Sol, Najva
What is Cultural Appropriation, And How Can You Avoid It?
A Practical Wedding Blog
http://apracticalwedding.com/2016/02/what-is-cultural-appropriation-definition-examples/
Feb-16

Abdul-Jabbar, Kareem
Cornrows and Cultural Appropriation: The Truth About Racial Identity Theft
Time Magazine http://time.com/4011171/cornrows-and-cultural-appropriation-the-truth-about-racial-identity-theft/
Aug-15

Garcia, Feliks
Alt-right vs White Supremacist: What is the difference?
The Independent (UK)
http://www.independent.co.uk/news/world/americas/alt-right-white-supremacist-whats-the-difference-donald-trump-steve-bannon-president-elect-a7417486.html
Nov-16

Jackson, Harold
The Legacy of W.E.B. DuBois and the NAACP
Philadelphia Inquirer
http://www.philly.com/philly/columnists/harold_jackson/20150712_The_legacy_of_W_E_B__DuBois_and_the_NAACP.html
Jul-15

Elias, Marilyn
The School-to-Prison Pipeline
Indiana University
http://www.indiana.edu/~pbisin/docs/School_to_Prison.pdf
Spring 2013

Sanchez, Adam
What We Don't Learn About the Black Panther Party--but Should
Huffington Post http://www.huffingtonpost.com/the-zinn-education-project/what-we-dont-learn-about_b_12572590.html
Oct-16

Coates, Ta-Nehisi
The Case for Reparations
The Atlantic
http://www.theatlantic.com/magazine/archive/2014/06/the-case-for-reparations/361631/

Coates, Ta-Nehisi
The Black Family in the Age of Incarceration
The Atlantic
http://www.theatlantic.com/magazine/archive/2015/10/the-black-family-in-the-age-of-mass-incarceration/403246/

McFarland, Melanie
History repeating: PBS' 'Black America Since MLK' shows progress made and lost
Salon Magazine http://www.salon.com/2016/11/15/history-repeating-pbss-black-america-since-mlk-shows-progress-made-and-lost/
Oct-16

Onion, Rebecca
Is Racism a Disease?
Slate Magazine
http://www.slate.com/articles/news_and_politics/history/2016/11/is_racism_a_psychological_disorder.html
Nov-16

Carten, Alma
How Slavery's Legacy Affects the Mental Health of Black Americans
The New Republic
https://newrepublic.com/article/122378/how-slaverys-legacy-affects-mental-health-black-americans
Jul-15

www.ingramcontent.com/pod-product-compliance
Lightning Source LLC
Chambersburg PA
CBHW030256030426
42336CB00009B/407